ACCIDENTAL MILLIONAIRE

Also by Derrick Arnott:

Social Domestic & Pleasure: Volume I
Diadem Books 2011
ISBN 978-1-908026-22-4

ACCIDENTAL MILLIONAIRE

Volume II

Derrick Arnott

Volume II of Derrick Arnott's popular sorta' autobiography Social

Domestic & Pleasure.

The rise and fall of Arnott Insurance and Lloyds of London.

DIADEM BOOKS

ACCIDENTAL MILLIONAIRE: VOLUME II

Published by Diadem Books
Distribution coordination by Spiderwize

For information, please contact:

Diadem Books
16 Lethen View
Tullibody
Alloa
FK10 2GE UK

www.diadembooks.com

ISBN: 978-1-908026-30-9

For Liz, James, Tim, Jacob, their children… & theirs.

The author is a fool who, not content with those he lives with, insists on boring future generations.
Charles de Montesquieu, 1689 – 1755.

Contents

Acknowledgements

To all the people who have made it possible for this manuscript to survive beyond the pipe dream stage, I am indebted.

To Brian Sutherland and my mother who inspired the idea. To Mary Millen (Marilyn) Thomson who spent hours slaving over a hot typewriter. To Karen Flowers who pulled it all together into a printable format. To my family and friends.

To my wife who was one of the many people whose idiosyncrasies provided me with a wealth of material.

To New Writing North at Newcastle University whose support was so valuable and to Alan Wilkinson of The Literary Consultancy, for his professional critique of my work which rescued it from its original haphazard draft.

To my business associates from whom I learned so much and to my loyal staff whose dedication helped to make Arnotts, in its heyday, a major player in the car insurance market.

Thanks too, to all those characters, foes as well as friends, who have touched my life for better or for worse without whom it would have been a duller existence and not worth writing about.

And finally to Charles Muller, Joanne and the team at Diadem Books who were able to take my work in a manuscript format and transform it into a published finished article.

One

SOCIAL DOMESTIC & PLEASURE

Never judge a cover by its book.
Chrissarism

THIS WAS THE TITLE chosen for the author's first book about the *social, domestic, pleasurable (*and sometimes painful) experiences of a shy boy from a poor and often homeless family in Middlesbrough and his determination to heed his father's advice and "better himself". Advice which, in his efforts to do so, led him into a hasty marriage, divorce and custody nightmare, a deep religious experience, battles with authority, two narrow escapes from bankruptcy and ultimately, success and contentment.

The original manuscript included many chapters relating to the rise (and almost fall) of Arnott Insurance (We Arnott Insured), Lloyds of London and the interesting characters associated with business life, including the director who became famous as Chairman of Gretna Football Club. On the advice of his publisher and earlier The Literary Consultancy, those chapters were considered to include enough material to justify a second volume of his sorto' autobiography.

It cannot strictly be called a sequel to the first since, chronologically, its content relates to much of the period covered in Volume I and ideally perhaps they should be read in conjunction with each other. Nevertheless the general opinion is that even on its own it is a good read, even for those who are not interested in business or insurance, and especially for those who are. The title chosen for this book (which was originally "Unlikely Millionaire") is down partly to the author's unpretentious modesty and his opinion that much of the credit for his success as a businessman can be attributed to a few fortuitous events, since his motivation primarily was never to become rich, but rather to succeed in overcoming what he felt was the stigma of his background

Some names have been changed to avoid embarrassment, possible lawsuits and, for the sake of clarity, some of the early events recorded in Volume I are repeated here.

Here is the second part of his story.

♣

If you were to ask a thousand school leavers what their chosen career would be, it is highly unlikely that any would say "An insurance man". Insurance companies, therefore, must be content to recruit from rejects by other employers or from people desperate for a job. The problem is that insurance does not have the glamorous appeal of other careers and it is quite important for us to feel a bit of pride when we tell others what we do for a living, especially as young men as part of our chat up routine!

"Get a white collar job!" was the only bit of career advice I got from my father who had worked shifts in the local blast furnaces all his life and hoped that his son, who had emerged from Grammar School with six 'O'-levels (later called GCSE's), would "better himself."

Having failed an interview to become a draughtsman and with few "white collar" options available, I applied for a job with an insurance company called Road Transport & General because firstly, I thought it must have something to do with cars for which I had developed a fascination during my youth hostelling and hitch-hiking days, and secondly, I was getting desperate. This time I passed the interview, which in itself was a minor miracle since I was a nervous wreck and my parents owned nothing worth insuring – and couldn't have afforded the premium if they had – so consequently I didn't even know what insurance was! I was offered a job at a starting salary of £78 per annum which I gladly accepted, even if it was only as a junior clerk. R T & G must have been desperate too, though at £1.50 a week they had little to lose. Thus I stumbled into an insurance career more by accident than design. I am glad that I did, even though it made a liar out of me – I always boasted to my dates that I was a draughtsman!

Thanks to the patience and encouragement of my old bosses Bill Robertson, Wilf Boddy and later, when I was transferred to R T & G's regional branch in Newcastle, Mr L R Burton-Jenkins, my career blossomed and I quickly qualified as an Associate of the Chartered Insurance Institute. But my self-confidence was given a super-charged boost when I left RT&G and joined United British Insurance as a junior Inspector (insurance jargon for a rep).

Dick Geddes, my new boss at UB, had a huge influence on me. He could have sold sand to the Arabs. His story of the two shoe salesmen helped me to develop a positive approach to life and my lateral thinking mind processes which were to serve me so well in my career and indeed in my life generally.

The first shoe salesman was given the opportunity to go and work in Africa. Dismayed, he turned it down. "But they don't wear shoes in Africa," he complained. The second shoe salesman snapped up the chance to go. "What a fantastic opportunity!" he exclaimed. "All those potential customers!"

My new boss at UB, like a slave master, relentlessly drove his team of inspectors, insisting that they made twenty calls a day visiting their existing agents and canvassing new ones. He too was ambitious and promotion for him depended on achieving better results than his predecessor and the more dramatically and quickly this happened the better. I described in Volume I, how some of the other inspectors, used to a cushy number under their previous boss, and to whom this new regime was a shock to the system, resorted to cunning subterfuges to persuade Geddes that they were achieving their targets. John Naylor the senior Inspector, from always arriving at the office late, became the first to arrive. Not because he had suddenly found a new enthusiasm for work, but to open the daily post and extract from it anything pertaining to his agents – cheques, proposal forms and so on. He would then put them in his briefcase before going to the nearby Tatler Cinema Café for a coffee from which he could observe the entrance to the office. On seeing the boss arrive he would then return to the office and with a flourish in front of Geddes, would remove the documents which he had earlier planted there, pretending that he had collected them from his agents during his "calls" on them the previous day!

I didn't need to resort to such subterfuges. I was a devotee of Dick Geddes and with his encouragement my already intense enthusiasm became boundless. He was surely destined for stardom and I was, or so I thought, being swept along with him. This all changed when he burned himself out in an effort to impress those above him and in whose hands his future was held. He suffered a massive heart attack and the race for him was over. From this experience I learned a vicarious lesson which was soon to have an influence in another decision I was about to make.

It was one of the Dick Geddes inspired cold calls which was to again result in a change of career direction – and to change my life. This particular cold call was to a second-hand car sales plot at Monkwearmouth, Sunderland – Tommy Downey Motors. Tommy sold old bangers very cheaply and had a thriving business. Perhaps his main attribute was a charming ability to deal with complaints – of which there were many. Of course with such a vast turnover of cars there were lots of opportunities to sell car insurance which of course was compulsory. Unfortunately my premiums – or rather United British premiums – were uncompetitive, so Mr Geddes and I came up with a plan. We would allow Tommy to issue a thirty-day cover note for £1 or £2 and I would follow the case up by calling on the punter, filling in the forms and collecting the balance of the premium. This suited Tommy perfectly since he would, hassle free, receive 10% of the total premium, not just the deposit, so we did a lot of business together. Around this time, during my house-to-house calls, I came across many examples of the illogical impracticality which has its roots in old-fashioned working class pride. Even in the most overcrowded and squalid homes one room was always kept "for best" and used only on special occasions, which included visits from the insurance man, the rent man – and occasionally the bailiff! There was of course an inevitable bad debt problem but my new business figures looked good – and so did Dick Geddes's. Eventually we had to put an end to this arrangement and ask Tommy to collect the full premium or a more substantial deposit. He did his best for me but the local brokers, particularly Eric Matthews of Tyneside Scottish, could undercut our premiums by a considerable margin.

By then Tommy and I had become friends and I found myself on the fringe of a high society life in Sunderland. Tommy was making a lot of money and mixed with moneyed friends – all with exotic sports cars. I was in awe of them. They obviously liked me and included me in their escapades. Maybe it made them feel good to have someone like me looking up in awe at them. Illegal road racing and wild parties were the order of the day – and the night. I found this new lifestyle irresistible. Here I was, a lad from a prefab house on a council estate, mixing with High Society!

The young executive

Two

JACK REED

Life is about 10% what happens to you and 90% how you handle it.
Dolly Frankell

ONE DAY when I paid my regular visit to Monkwearmouth, there was a stranger in the office. He introduced himself as Jack Reed and he was there to help out Tommy with the paperwork and finances. We arranged to have a drink after work with Tommy and we got on very well. Jack was Tommy's brother-in-law and explained that he had lost his job as a Company Secretary when Whites Marine Engineering Company of Hebburn had gone into liquidation. As we chatted over a few beers Tommy had asked me why our premiums were so high and why those offered by Eric Matthews were lower.

"Well, Eric is a broker," I explained.

"Why aren't you one then?" asked Tommy. "We could give you loads of business if you were."

There was no answer to that save to say that I had a good job and good prospects.

"You won't make much money though," was Tommy's observation.

Jack's arrival on the scene changed things. He pursued with me the broker idea and I was warming to it. Jack of course had a motive. He was out of work looking for something to do which would make him some money and saw in me an opportunity to do so. We set up a pilot business in his office at Tommy Downey Motors. At that time NIG Insurance was the most competitive car insurance company but they would only grant agency facilities to established brokers. We were able to find a way round this by Jack applying for a sub agency through a large Birmingham broker – J.A. Harrison Ltd. This of course meant sharing the commission but at least it gave us a start. Jack was able to sign up most of Tommy's customers and build up a client base. When the time was right, I handed in my notice to United British and we opened a small, damp and occasionally waterlogged basement office in Frederick Street, Sunderland, under the name of Arnott Reed & Co. It was a three-way partnership between myself, Jack and Tommy. I took to the road to drum up business from other motor dealers and this coupled with responses to our advertising soon had the business on its feet. There were of course setbacks, born out of inexperience, but these were survived. We were then, as full time insurance brokers, able to apply for agencies with other competitive insurance companies and we quickly built up a good reputation for competitive car insurance.

Business is like baking. If you have the right ingredients in the right quantities and if you know how to cook, you will bake a good pie. In our case enough of the ingredients existed. Tommy had business experience, Jack had financial skills and I was a pretty good cook. A bit of good luck helps too. By a fortuitous coincidence which enabled us to indulge in a bit of plagiarism, there existed in Frederick Street Sunderland, a reputable and long established insurance firm called Leslie Arnott & Co and also the town's prominent legal practice Richard Reed & Co. Our names came in handy. By calling our Company Arnott Reed & Co we benefited from a bit of vicarious respectability. The timing (another important ingredient) was right too and I gradually had to scale down my motor trade connections to concentrate on dealing with the ever increasing number of new clients we were attracting to our office counter which, to save money, I had built myself with some old wood I had found, thereby demonstrating a further ingredient for business success – frugality.

I don't know what happened between Jack and Tommy but I was persuaded by Jack to ditch Tommy and form a new 50/50 company Arnott & Reed (Insurance) Ltd. I was uneasy about the morals of this but went along with it on Jack's insistence that Tommy's reputation was not good for the business. I suspect the truth was a recognition by Jack that our business had the potential to make a lot of money and that his motive may have been to get his hands on half of it and not just a third.

I didn't lack enthusiasm when working for United British. Working for myself it was almost excessive. Jack and I would stand shoulder to shoulder at our small basement counter dealing with queues of customers as our reputation for cheap premiums and good professional service grew. In Jack, like Dick Geddes, I had another elder mentor to help me to develop my business skills. On one particularly busy Saturday morning I was to learn from Jack a particularly important business lesson. In my enthusiasm to provide a tiptop personal service to our customers I would devote to them however much time they wanted. Mr McCririck had, after much persuasion and reassurance from me, finally taken out insurance on his moped and reluctantly paid me his premium of twelve shillings and sixpence, out of which we would earn, gross, about one shilling. He then went on to ask me for insurance quotes for a series of motorcars with which he may at some time in the future replace his moped. Each quote was received with little enthusiasm and often with derision. I could sense that Jack was becoming agitated as he dealt with a stream of customers and when at last he was free he spun round on Mr McCririck and asked him if he was happy with our quote. Before he had time to moan again Jack asked me how much he had paid, then put his hand into his own pocket, pulled out twelve shillings and sixpence, thrust it across the counter and told Mr McCririck that if he didn't like it he could f**k off! I was horrified. In my naïve and idealistic mind this was no way to treat customers. Later Jack explained to me how we were there to run a business and make money – not to pander to moaning bastards like Mr McCririck who in one hour had earned us one shilling whilst Jack had dealt with a dozen customers and collected £100. I got the message, one that has stood me in good stead ever since. Mr

McCririck got the message too. He fled with his covernote and became a loyal and trouble free customer for many years thereafter.

Jack and I worked well together in those days. We enjoyed the customer contact in the front line of the business and our customers enjoyed the personal service we offered and on the back of mainly personal recommendation the business flourished – at least in the sense that we attracted more and more customers, one of whom, a Mr Joseph Edward Laidler, was to become a close friend and my business partner in Tenerife many years later. Jack and I became in a sense, victims of our own success. Our working day was taken up entirely with client contact and we had little time to process the paperwork which would pile up and which had to be done after hours. The office hours were determined by pub opening times. Jack was traditionally an early hours barfly and nothing would be allowed to interfere with his opening time sessions in the Palatine Hotel. It fell to me therefore to stay behind to catch up on the essential paperwork. I didn't mind. But my wife did.

It wasn't long before we needed bigger premises and in 1962 we moved along the street from No 11 to new street level premises at No 22 Frederick Street where we didn't need the mop and bucket or wellies which were kept in the old office for rainy days. We were able also to buy a company car which I had the exclusive use of since Jack did not drive. He did take several tests but failed each one due, he said, to being too nervous, which was strange since in every other respect he appeared extremely self-confident. I didn't complain. It suited me fine to keep the Austin A40 to myself. We also employed a young girl, Eva, to do the typing and filing. Jack teased her unmercifully. On her first day she was sent round to buy a compluffer for the A40 from Halfords who needless to say sent her back empty handed, so I sketched out a rude picture and sent her back to Halfords to show them what a compluffer looked like. Poor lass. Yes, the early days of Arnott Insurance were fun.

Jack Reed, whose worries were by no means behind him.

Three

V & G

MY EARLY BUSINESS DAYS were fresh and exciting. The whole new world of commerce was opening up for me and I continued to be fascinated by the new and 'important' people I was meeting. Colourful characters were plentiful. Our clients included Vince Landau of 'One Armed Bandit' fame who fled the country when his infamous scam was unearthed, although I have to say that in my opinion he wasn't a crook, just someone who saw an opportunity to make a lot of money and exploit the gullibility and greed of his victims. You don't make money without being sharp witted and streetwise. Mr Landau's company based in Sunderland supplied gaming machines. They were called One Armed Bandits in those days because to activate them you had to pull down on a lever at the side of the machine. They were popular in seaside fun parlours but had not yet been introduced into pubs and clubs. Enter Mr Landau and Co with what I believe was an extremely clever proposition for, mainly, working men's clubs of which there were many hundreds in the North East of England.

The suggestion was that the clubs should buy the machines but the cost was often prohibitive since the mark up on them was high –

ridiculously and intentionally so. This of course is where the big profit was made. "Not a problem," the salesman would say. "All you need is a deposit of ten per cent and the instalments will be paid by us out of the takings" – and sure enough it worked. The clubs were making money, Landau's company was making money and no doubt the collectors who emptied the machines would be having their fiddles too – probably in cahoots with the club stewards. I don't have the details of what exactly went wrong but I guess Mr Landau and his associates became greedy after they had saturated the market with machines, from the sale of which they would have made enormous profits. Payments to the Hire Purchase companies began to fall into arrears, no doubt because the takings from the machines were being pocketed. There was nothing the clubs could do about it. They had signed the Hire Agreement and they and not Mr Landau's company were responsible for keeping up the payments. Needless to say the promise by Landau to make the payments out of the money collected was a verbal one and therefore legally unenforceable. The Hire Purchase companies were protected by their right of repossession so they didn't suffer. The clubs just had to bite the bullet.

On the subject of scams, an Irishman calling himself Patrick John Quill was introduced to Jack and me one day in the Palatine Bar. He had recently arrived in Sunderland and set up a car sales operation in Tatham Street where he was doing remarkably well. We too were soon doing well on the back of his success. Because of our social life Jack and I had become fairly well connected in the local commercial fraternity, one of our drinking partners being the area manager of a finance company, who, unusually, had agreed to give us an agency from which we earned fifteen per cent of the hire charges from each agreement. I say 'unusually' because agencies were normally available only to bona fide motor traders. Jack and I hatched up quite a lucrative side-line to insurance. We would buy the *Sunderland Echo* every afternoon and contact all the advertisers with cars for sale, offering their buyers a hire purchase option, thus facilitating their sale. We had no difficulty in persuading Mr Quill to use our facility and soon received a steady stream of agreements from him too. We did think it was a little odd that he wasn't interested in the commission but were not to know that he had bigger fish to fry. Our other motor trader friends shared our astonishment at the number of cars he was selling and what made it more puzzling was that all the cars were well over "book" price. We didn't ask any questions. The unexpected boost to our income was very welcome. One night several weeks later we had a drink in the Palatine with Patrick John Quill and that was the last we, or anyone else, saw of him. He'd done a runner.

Financial institutions are not streetwise. They are no match for the Patrick John Quills of this world. Every so often they lead with their chins – then cry "foul" when someone accepts the invitation and punches. Martins (now Barclays) Bank in Chester Road (my own bank, even now) were the fall guys. They were offering no deposit unsecured loans – a recipe for disaster. They did carefully look at each application but could find nothing wrong with Mr Quill's punters, even those on very low incomes. We were told that some were even unemployed. After all, if they had been able to save up a fifty per cent deposit to put down on a car then they must surely be thrifty people. The bank was not to know that the "deposit" was being borrowed on hire purchase. Few of the punters bothered to pay any instalments and the HP Company had to repossess just about every car sold. Nobody paid Martins Bank either – and they had no security to fall back on. They too assumed that they were taking on thrifty borrowers who had saved up a hefty deposit. In the end the Bank and the Finance Company came to an agreement to share their losses. In the meantime there were dozens of happy motorists who had, for a few months, the use of motor cars they would not otherwise have been able to afford and it hadn't cost them a penny. Even the insurance had been put on hire purchase. The punters were happy and so was Mr Quill who, by the time the excrement hit the fan, was presumably back in Ireland or maybe sunning himself and supping Sangria in Spain. Or maybe in some other town with the same scam using a different bank and finance company. When the punters were questioned they all said the same thing: "Mr Quill told me that all I had to do was to sign the forms and use the car for a few months and not bother paying anything." No doubt the bankers, already on fat salaries, would have been paid handsome bonuses for doing what must be the easiest job in the world – lending people money!

OK, the two characters I have just described could be accused of unethical activities, but not illegal ones. I learned a lot from these experiences. If you leave a loophole in the business procedures you put in place, you can be sure that someone will exploit it and if they do, then make sure they don't take you for much.　My company had suffered from bad debts and pilfering of course but because we dealt with a lot of clients paying small amounts rather than a few large clients we were able to survive the occasional losses that got through the net. We did lose several thousand pounds at Sunderland once when one of our front line customer contact girls was drafted temporarily into the accounts department and was able to cleverly remove the cash and the audit trail for a while. She tried to protest wrongful dismissal but the police were involved and the tribunal couldn't be held until the police had concluded their investigations which in fact they never did. The evidence was quite simple and clear but they just couldn't get their heads round it. Fraud investigations are not the most successful of police operations.　Amazingly, the girl in question some years later asked us for a reference! We suggested that her new employer should telephone us!

I was annoyed with the girl of course. But I was also annoyed with myself for failing to ensure that temptation was not put in her way, which I believe is the duty of responsible management. Our systems and procedures were changed to avoid a recurrence.

With my boundless enthusiasm and under Jack's mature guidance, the business was flourishing and I was keen to take advantage of the market which existed then. There were no motor brokers in Darlington and we opened a branch there. Jack I think was less keen but I pushed him into agreeing. In truth I wanted to prove that I could run an office without Jack. We still worked well together but there were certain things that disturbed me. Even though the company was set up with a fifty-fifty shareholding I felt that Jack regarded me as a junior partner. He controlled the purse strings and would carry around with him the day's takings which by then were substantial. It wouldn't have been so bad if he had gone straight home. Instead, he would have his opening time session in the Palatine – a session which often lasted until closing time, after which he would sometimes be persuaded by the later arrivals at the bar to go night clubbing. Jack was a gambler too, always claiming how successful his visits to the bookies and the roulette tables had been. Every year at audit time there were cash discrepancies. I'm not suggesting that Jack was deliberately dishonest but in view of his lifestyle may perhaps have been careless or forgetful from time to time. He would hear nothing of my suggestion that we should arrange night safe deposit facilities with the bank so when he went on holiday once, I myself arranged this facility only for Jack to discontinue the practice on his return. Cracks began to appear in our working relationship.

In 1967 Jack had the first of a series of heart attacks. He was a tough old cookie and survived – once by plunging himself into a cold bath. Not very pleasant for Jack of course, but his input into the business was then much reduced and we had to sell off the Darlington business so that I could concentrate on Sunderland. My ambitions for expansion were thwarted – at least for the time being. I urged Jack to take it easy assuring him that I could run the show. I was even looking forward to being in control. Jack however was stubborn. He had other ideas. This created more frustration. I had the responsibility without the decision-making autonomy, a situation which can be quite stressful, as many a football manager will tell you.

I was no longer at that time the carefree young man of a couple of years previously. I was married with a mortgage and, when daughter Liz was born, an extra mouth to feed and new responsibilities. This situation didn't last long but instead of getting better it got worse – much worse. At the time Jack was having his heart attacks my marriage was falling apart. In 1968 when problems at work were at their worst I was at the same time trying to cope with my horrendous domestic situation which resulted in a separation and culminated in divorce. Fortunately by then we had taken on extra staff, notably Geraldine Robertson, Ian Fletcher and Dave Smith. Ian was in fact my wife's cousin though that had nothing to do with his appointment.

1971 was a landmark year for Arnott & Reed and the events of that year and subsequently were to have a big influence on the future direction of the company. As one of the area's leading motor brokers we were then able to obtain agency facilities with all the competitive insurance companies and whilst this had proved to be a two-edged sword when a few of them collapsed, we had built up a massive account with Vehicle General Insurance Company, whose premiums were very competitive but just as importantly, the V&G were members of the BIA – The British Insurance Association – which endowed them with respectability and, we assumed, some policyholder protection. This was important so that confidence in the market could be restored after a series of insurance company failures – London and Cheshire, Midland Northern and Scottish and famously Emil Savundra's Fire Auto & Marine who we initially refused to represent but were reluctantly forced into taking the agency because we were losing a lot of customers seeking very cheap premiums and finding them through rival brokers. In an effort to dissuade customers from taking FAM policies we insisted that they sign disclaimers absolving us from responsibility should they go bust. We thought this would put them off. It didn't. They signed of course – anything to save a few bob – and it was amazing how many angry customers came into our office blaming us and denying that they had signed disclaimers – even when we produced them for inspection. Why do people buy insurance in such a different way to other products? Fortunately we were not too heavily involved with FAM. Not so in the case of V&G.

On the evening of the Second of March 1971 I watched the announcement on the six o'clock news with incredulity. Vehicle & General Insurance Co Ltd were in liquidation. Policyholders were advised not to drive their cars and to seek immediate replacement cover.

In preparation for the onslaught, I went straight back to the office, sneaking in so that I wouldn't be waylaid by any early bird complainants. I stayed there all night and though knowing nothing of the circumstances, I typed up a hastily prepared 'explanation' with a timed tear-off deposit slip. Using our old Gestetner duplicating machine, expecting it to die on me at any moment, I laboriously made two thousand copies. By this expedient we were able over the next few days, to handle in a reasonably orderly fashion, the constant queues of customers stretching into and along the pavement of Frederick Street. They would receive an acknowledgment of their payment, often as little as £2, and confirmation that they were then 'on cover' and that a cover note would be sent to them through the post. Half the staff would man the counter, the other would work in the back office processing the paperwork and answering telephone calls. Jack jumped on a train to London with a suitcase and came back from Milestone Motor Policies at Lloyds with it full of cover note books. I booked into a local B&B to be close to the action and to focus totally on the job in hand and we all worked tirelessly day and night under tremendous pressure. We were all exhausted but we survived. In fact, we did better than survive, since up to two thousand customers would pay us twice that year which financed the purchase and extension of larger premises, again in Frederick Street (No. 6).

When the dust settled and I was able to take stock of the situation there were some questions to be asked. One of the reasons we had placed so many clients with V&G was that they were members of the BIA. I thought it a little odd that some of the other local BIA companies were quick to offer the services of their local reps who, from shortly after our office opened on day one, stood shoulder to shoulder with us at our counter (and I learned later, at similar counters up and down the country) and persuaded many of our clients to re-insure with their particular company. It was all too slick and well organised. I was suspicious. Did these companies have prior knowledge? Indeed, did they have a hand in the V&G demise? V&G were certainly a threat to the mainstream insurance establishment whose policyholders were deserting in their droves to take out policies with the first insurance company to offer 60% no claims bonus and to introduce the step back system whereby one claim would not mean a total loss of no claims bonus and therefore a huge increase in premium, but instead a partial loss – from 60% to 40% – so as not to penalise too harshly careful drivers for one mishap. In addition a driver's full no claims bonus would remain intact after a non-fault accident. V&G had refused to be a party to the knock-for-knock arrangement to which every other BIA company subscribed. V&G justified their decision on the grounds that since they had a portfolio of careful drivers only, then they were likely to have fewer fault accidents so why should they share the claims costs? Yes, V&G as pioneers were a threat and when you threaten the establishment you had better watch your back!

I was grateful to my new wife Chris for her support during this difficult time and I was so proud of my staff who had worked tirelessly day and night under tremendous pressure. I treated them to a well-deserved dinner at the Roker Hotel and vowed then that they would share in the future success of the company. We had a team to beat the world!

Four

A PEOPLE BUSINESS

I've come to believe that each of us has a personal calling that's as unique as a fingerprint –
and that the best way to succeed is to discover what you do best and then to offer it to others in
the form of service, working hard and also allowing the energy of the universe to lead you.
Oprah Winfrey

I N THE 1970s INSURANCE, and many others, were businesses which prided themselves on customer service. Sadly technology has now changed all that. It isn't easy to speak to a real person these days and almost impossible to do so face to face. I now spend hours of my time with a telephone in my hand listening to a recorded robot telling me what options I have, none of which ever seem to include the one I want, except the one to speak to a customer service representative, only then to be informed by the recorded robot that they are all busy with other customers and I should hold on, often at premium rate, or call back later. When I do call back the procedure is repeated and the recorded robot tells me how important my call is and that a rep will speak to me as soon as possible. The robot then puts on a tape of some music that is supposed to soothe me but after fifteen minutes or so, during which time the robot has repeated fifteen times how important my call is, it's beginning to irritate me to death so I hang up and stomp around in a bad mood for hours. And what about the Sunderland man who left his specs in the local branch of his bank? Calling the bank to see if they were there he got to talk to a lady from Kuala Lumpur. Needless to say, she didn't know. Nor did she know the number of the branch but she wasn't allowed to divulge it even if she did. Customer service? They haven't a clue!

While I'm in chuntering mode I might as well have a go at complaining about the so-called complaints services which have been set up as a knee jerk reaction in an attempt by Government to convince us that they are concerned about our frustrations with Twenty-First Century service and are doing something about it. Have you ever tried to use one of these 'services'? There are apparently lots of them with offices usually in London (no expense spared here) and manned by highly paid staff with nothing to do. The reason they have nothing to do was revealed in a survey carried out which found that only 3% of the population knew of their existence or how they could contact them. Oh, how I would love the job of shaking up this shambolic, inefficient state of affairs. I would start by relocating these quangos to cheaper perhaps centralised headquarters in regions of high unemployment and publicise one simple national number which we could contact to obtain the numbers of the appropriate body to whom we could address our complaint. Or is that too simple?

It was cool rational thinking and our customer service skills which had rescued us from what could have proved a disastrous time for our company in the 1970's as many of the big insurance companies attempted to capitalise on our difficulties at V&G time by mounting intensive marketing campaigns to persuade motorists to deal direct with them. They failed then because they lacked customer service skills, which at least in those days were valued by the motoring public.

Let me explain the nature of our role as insurance brokers to those who don't already know and to those who do but do not appreciate it. Our job was to compare the products and prices of various insurance companies and select the best to recommend to our clients. There was once a time when nearly all insurance companies had the same premiums and policies but the 'tariff' as they called it and which was what amounted to a cartel, was disbanded in the nineteen-sixties shortly after my Company was established. This paved the way for open competition and premiums varied widely between insurers. The premium wasn't the only criteria we had to consider. Apart from the price and quality of the policy there was the question of the level of commission we received, some insurers paying as high as 20% of premium and some as low as 7.5%. Usually, but not always, the insurers offering the lowest commissions also offered the lowest premiums but an increasing number of insurers, to avoid the massive cost of direct marketing, were making their policies available only through brokers to whom they paid a higher rate of commission in return for us doing the admin work at which we were pretty good. Our efficiency coupled with the volume of business we were generating enabled us to deal with a wide range of insurers out of which we were able to offer our clients a wide range of products and prices. We were therefore extremely competitive. The selection process in these pre-computer days wasn't as easy as it sounds and required a great deal of experience, market knowledge and skill. We were pretty good in these areas too. The more alternative insurers we had to choose from the more difficult became the task, but the more competitive we became. In order to get agencies with some of the more competitive insurers I was required to sign personal guarantees. Why don't our stupid governments and public services insist on such safeguards before awarding lucrative contracts to private companies whose directors, with personal impunity, irresponsibly squander tax payers money then pay themselves bonuses and perks before allowing their companies to go into liquidation for tax payers to pick up the pieces?

My determination always to give our customers the best deal irrespective of what was in it for us, wasn't always shared by Jack but it certainly paid dividends not only during this period but also during the expansion which followed and during some difficult trading conditions which all Companies have to face from time to time. For us to gain access to the competitive premiums available through Lloyds syndicates for instance, it was mandatory to operate through a Lloyds Broker with whom we had to share commission. None of our competitors dealt with Lloyds for this reason. That's the way Lloyds was, and still is, set up. Much of our V&G business was replaced with Lloyds syndicates, thanks to Jack's trip to London with his suitcase. Not only were Lloyds premiums competitive, we were able to boast a guarantee that they could not and would not go bust, which was important at that time of uncertainty in the minds of the motoring public. Before its image was tarnished by the scandals of the eighties and nineties, of which I was personally to become a victim, the name Lloyds was synonymous with respectability and security. So, in the wake of the V&G collapse we found ourselves in a very strong position with our reputation only slightly tarnished and with a wider range of agencies than our competitors. In addition we had a staff who had proved themselves to be competent, enthusiastic and loyal.

It was clear to me that we should take advantage of the position in which we then found ourselves. It was my opinion that if we did not provide a career path for our young ambitious staff then we would inevitably lose them. I proposed to Jack that we should perhaps consider expanding the company by opening a new branch. I had in mind as manager, Dave Smith for whom Jack didn't have a lot of time and whose future at Arnott & Reed was uncertain. OK, he was young and brash but he was talented too and I took the view that our relationships with staff should be commercially objective not personal. Jack wouldn't hear of it. "We've got more business than we can cope with," was his response. "We could do with less business, not more." It was OK for Jack who was then approaching sixty but not for me and I told him so. He didn't take it well. "You do what you want," he said, "we are not expanding and that's that." I could not believe what I was hearing. I was prepared to take on board all the responsibility, allow Jack to become almost a sleeping partner – or at least to have an easy stress-free life on equal pay and benefits to me – and enjoy a 50% stake in an expanding company with lots of potential. Jack unfortunately didn't see it that way which I found extremely frustrating, which is what 50/50 business partnerships usually are – like marriage but worse. You have all the responsibilities and problems you have in a marriage – and you don't get your leg over!

When I had become a partner in Arnott Reed & Co in 1959 it wasn't like going into business. Jack took responsibility for and controlled all matters financial and I just did a job. I had become a businessman by accident rather than by design – at least not my design since it was Jack and Tommy Downey who had persuaded me, not without some reluctance on my part, to abandon my cosy zone at United British with its clearly defined career path. However there was nothing accidental about the next big step I was about to take, though again it was taken with some reluctance.

A few months before the collapse of V&G I had remarried. I had custody of my daughter and another child was on the way. Thanks to my new wife Chris who, before we married, had spent a long time looking after young daughter Liz, my domestic scene was settled and happy – another ingredient for success in business – and I was once more in control of my life. Business decisions could be made rationally rather than expediently.

Stung by his attitude and his remarks I took Jack at his word, rented a small office in Baker Street, Middlesbrough and applied for agencies in the name of V C Marshall & Co (my new wife's maiden name). I don't know why I didn't use my own name. Perhaps I felt a little guilty about deserting Jack despite his attitude. Shortly afterwards I registered the company and changed the name to Marshall Arnott Ltd.

Jack's dislike of Dave Smith was becoming more obvious and I think he was relieved when I 'head hunted' him to take charge at Middlesbrough, even though this was to put extra pressure on the remaining Sunderland staff, but Jack was oblivious to the problems on the front line in which he didn't ever involve himself, being content to sit in his office upstairs and 'count the money'.

The V&G had recruited well and after 02.03.71 many experienced insurance personnel found themselves out of work which enabled me to recruit Dennis Mee as Dave's assistant at the Middlesbrough branch which quickly established itself and grew rapidly. I was now really in business on my own! A couple of years later I found another ex-V&G man working in the area. Iain Ferguson had held a quite senior position in their underwriting department in Gateshead and I resumed my acquaintance with him and his wife Pat with whom Chris too became quite friendly. I introduced Iain to my good friend Brian

Sutherland and as fellow Scots, Glaswegians in fact, they soon formed a friendship particularly as they both favoured the blue half of their native city. As well as becoming a good friend Iain became in my mind something else too – an ingredient in my plans for expansion.

In 1973 our next branch was opened in Portland Terrace, Newcastle, with Iain installed as manager. This too became a busy branch with for some reason a predominance of civil servants as clients – probably to do with the big DHSS centre in Longbenton. Along with schoolteachers they are not, we had discovered, the easiest of customers to please. To make matters worse many insurers offered them discounted premiums – and reduced our commission for the privilege!

At that time premiums were rising steeply, partly due to inflation but also because of the influx of foreign, mainly Japanese, cars into the market. These were very keenly priced and boasted all sorts of extras not provided by British manufacturers. Clearly the plan was to flood the market, weaken the competition, gain a foothold and make their profit from the sale of spare parts which were twice and often three or more times the price of their British counterparts. This led later to the introduction of car groupings by insurance companies who originally charged premiums according to horse power and later, engine size. Our clients could not understand and often refused to accept, the extra premium imposed when changing from a British car to a Japanese one of similar size and our staff often had to suffer abuse at the hands of the loud mouth, bully section of our client base. To help them to deal with this I researched and documented the comparative cost of various parts so that they could demonstrate the justification for the higher premiums. But there are some customers who are totally unreasonable and unmanageable, like Mr Ogilvy, a civil servant of course, who gave Iain's assistant Anfre Levinson a hard time after his renewal premium had increased. He hadn't made a claim so why should he pay more – this despite the soaring inflation at the time. He, like many others, resented paying for something he didn't want or need because he never had accidents. It was only the fact that car insurance was compulsory and he needed it to tax his car that forced him to take out insurance. This wasn't Anfre's fault of course but ignorant people like that don't consider such things. Comprehensive insurance isn't compulsory but when you suggest to these people that they could cut their costs by 50% by taking third party insurance they don't want to know. "Why not?" we would say. "I thought you said you never had accidents." But these people are not just unreasonable, they are irrational too.

Mr Ogilvy was going to expose us. He would write to the press – and his MP etc. etc. When these tactics failed to reduce his premium he demanded his proof of no claims bonus, vowed never to insure with us again and stormed out of the office. In fact, Mr Ogilvy's premium was, we knew, unbeatable. His insurer, Milestone Motor Policies, had in fact not applied their latest increase to existing policyholders. We were well rid of him. Mr Ogilvy however had other ideas. Having failed to find a cheaper quote he had the audacity to come back and demand that we renewed his policy with Milestone. Anfre refused. He was furious. We were he claimed, wrongly of course, breaking the law by refusing to insure him and he would report us. For the few shillings more it would have cost him elsewhere he was prepared to humiliate himself. He banged his money on the counter. Anfre stood her ground. He pushed it towards her. She pushed it back. Iain came out to see what the fuss was about and when his patience was exhausted he pushed the money onto the floor where Mr Ogilvy had to grovel for it before storming out, hurling abuse and threatening that we hadn't heard the last of it. We had. Loud mouths and bullies like him rarely have the guts to carry out their threats which is a pity because I rather enjoy taking them on. We didn't need those clients – the 10% who cause 90% of the trouble and work, and who invariably pay us the lowest premiums. But how could we identify them? A few years later the girls in Glasgow branch came up with a plan, which we adopted to score a lot of 4 (later 6) pointers!

Three of Arnotts' long serving girls on Geordie Nite duty.
L – R. Joan Harker, Gerry Burge and Jan Kennedy.

Five

HELLO GLASGOW, FAREWELL JACK

The best laid schemes o' mice and men
Gang aft agley
An' lea' e us naught but grief an' pain
For promis'd joy
Robert Burns (To a mouse) **1785**

A **MAJOR FACTOR** in assessing car insurance premiums is the density of traffic in which cars are used and Glasgow premiums were and still are among the highest in the country. With my Scottish connections it seemed therefore a logical step to consider Glasgow as a location for a branch of Marshall Arnott Ltd. With rents and overheads only slightly higher than in the North East and with premiums, and therefore our commissions, much higher, the potential for profit was obvious. The idea was taking shape. My philosophy was and still is that having started with an idea you progress it step by step. Push the next door and if it opens and no obstacles are revealed within then go in and push the next door and so on. The next step was to push the 'premises' door so after some initial groundwork Iain and I, taking advantage of the British Rail Travel and Stay deals they were promoting, booked into the North British Hotel at Queen Street Station. These deals had recently been kind to me. On a cheap trip to London with Chris our seat numbers had been selected in a lucky draw and we had won two first class tickets to anywhere in the UK. We chose Mousehole (pronounced Mousel) in Cornwall and had just returned from a wonderful trip there, staying in the posh Waterside Hotel where, a little out of our depth, we rubbed shoulders with the rich and famous.

Having deposited our luggage in our Glasgow hotel room Iain and I walked a couple of hundred metres up George Street to view the first and nearest potential site on our list. It was ideal. We cancelled the remaining appointments and spent three days on an expenses paid jaunt. I felt quite at home in the city of my ancestors. The motor superintendent of Provincial Insurance, an ex-colleague and friend of Iain Ferguson was head hunted to become our branch manager.

Only two more doors left. The first was to make sure that the insurers we dealt with would be happy to do business in Glasgow which was regarded as a high risk area and remote from London and Essex where many of the insurers were based. Many were reluctant to give us agency facilities but luckily and crucially, some of our favourite and most competitive insurers, including some Lloyds syndicates, who had no representation there, agreed to support us which gave us that competitive edge so useful when breaking new ground. Now I had enough ingredients to bake a Scotch pie!

I hope I am not being immodest by saying that I have always been ahead of the game when it comes to marketing. A start was made by promoting ourselves by way of a substantial leaflet distribution, featuring premiums from as little as nine pound something and with a £2 off voucher which engendered enough enquiries to give us an opportunity to show what we were made of. We also placed a half page ad in Yellow Pages, which was then in its infancy but whose potential I recognised. When our competitors followed suit, saturated that medium and pushed up the price we reduced our exposure and used the advertising budget in another direction. By then we had more than a foothold in the market with most of our enquiries coming from personal recommendation. Glasgow was an instant success story.

In those pre-computer and word processor days when clients enjoyed personal and individual correspondence it was necessary for us to find a good typist. The final door was pushed open. The response to our advertisement was encouraging. A short list of ten was selected and interviews arranged at which all the applicants were given a typing test. Only one got the spelling of "seperate" correct, a Mary Millen

Thomson, which made the selection easy. Though divorced she assured me that she had no family commitments and therefore would have no difficulty working full time. Years later she confessed to me that her family commitments were much more onerous than she had led me to believe. I too had a confession to make. I had later discovered that "seperate" was actually spelt **separate** and that she was in fact the only interviewee who had got it wrong! We were subsequently to become a good team and Marilyn, as she was popularly known, rose to the position of Group Motor Underwriting Manager and local shareholder and director. Who knows what dizzy heights she may have attained had she been able to spell! I believe I am more than a match for anyone when it comes to spelling and I can hardly believe that I got it wrong on this occasion. But "pobody's nerfect" – and our mutual poor grasp of the English language proved to be providential. Two years later Marilyn assumed control of the branch when some irregularities were discovered and the manager resigned. Many years later she was invited to type this manuscript for me and I think you will agree made an excellent job of it.

With total autonomy as the major shareholder at Marshall Arnott Ltd I had the freedom to introduce the working practices, staff training programmes and incentive schemes denied to me at Arnott & Reed, with the result that within five years my Company's turnover had exceeded what it had taken Arnott & Reed twenty years to achieve. I was keen to get control at Sunderland where the potential was obvious but I continued to be frustrated by Jack's intransigence. Another problem was that the staff there were beginning to get restless, aware as they were, of the better working conditions and rewards at the Marshall Arnott offices. I approached Jack again to discuss a possible buyout but he didn't give me any encouragement. We did however eventually sit down and put a value on the company of £100,000 so I offered him half of that – i.e. in proportion to our shareholding. Several months passed and whilst I was anxious to conclude a deal I didn't want to appear too desperate. But I was becoming impatient. There were signs of unrest, even rebellion, among the Arnott & Reed Sunderland staff who could not understand why the staff at Marshall

Arnott who they considered as colleagues were so much better off than they were. They were unaware of the politics going on upstairs. I feared that some may abandon ship and seek jobs elsewhere. I had of course earlier held on to Dave Smith by giving him the manager's job at Middlesbrough without which he would have surely left or been forced out by Jack, but it wasn't that easy with the others.

When Jack did eventually talk to me it was to say that he was considering an offer for his shares from a company in Leeds whose name he could not divulge and that they had offered him a higher price. To call his bluff, if indeed it was one, I wrote to him offering to sell him my 50% for £50,000, which would enable him to get an even better price from his 'buyer' in Leeds. I was by then half hoping that he would go for this proposition. My patience had been exhausted. Why should I, in the light of Jack's attitude, pay anything at all for what in effect was goodwill which I alone had created? I put the wheels in motion to open another branch of Marshall Arnott in Sunderland in direct competition to Arnott & Reed creating the bizarre situation of being in competition with myself! Offices close to the existing ones were acquired and the key Arnott & Reed employees were primed to join me as and when required. Their customers, or most of them, would surely have followed.

At the eleventh hour Jack capitulated and agreed to our original deal. I was now in a quandary since it was a simple matter to progress the alternative plan in which event I would have finished up with most of the Arnott & Reed client base for nothing. Not for the first or the last time in my life I did the honourable thing rather than the commercially sensible thing and I did the deal with Jack. Or was it the honourable thing? After all Jack all those years ago had squeezed out Tommy Downey who didn't get a penny for his original share in the partnership and I suppose in a sense, justice would have been done had I taken the hard line and told Jack to get lost. The consolation I can gain from making this 'commercial error' and from similar decisions in the future both personal and business which have cost me dearly, is that no-one has ever, or can ever, point the finger at me and say, "There's a man without integrity."

Six

WE ARNOTT INSURED

Half the time spent on training was probably wasted.
I wish I'd known which half.
D.A.

I HAD REMARRIED on 2nd January 1971 and moved to Middlesbrough, just two months before the V&G crash and it was in no small part due to the stability this brought to my life that I was able with confidence to devote more quality time to my business, or should I say businesses, since after setting up my new company Marshall Arnott Ltd I continued to manage Arnott & Reed in Sunderland because Jack was not capable of doing so since his heart attacks. He was obviously aware of what I was doing but the subject was never mentioned. Perhaps he was hoping that without his involvement my new company would fail. This couldn't have been further from the truth. Despite the fact that my new company was going from strength to strength and demanded my attention, I was still entirely loyal to Sunderland and devoted most of my time there. Perhaps if I hadn't, then Jack might have capitulated sooner but a big part of my heart was there and I couldn't bring myself to neglect what I considered was my duty to the old company and its workforce. Nothing it seemed could halt the progress of the two companies. But I was wrong.

As I said earlier much of this success was attributable to my new wife Chris's contribution at home but, ironically, it was the absence of this support domestically which was to cause a major setback commercially. It wasn't her fault of course. In 1976 after the birth of our third son Jacob, she suffered badly from post-natal depression followed by a hysterectomy and then a spinal disc replacement.

The events of this difficult period in my life were described in detail in Volume I – how I had no choice other than to neglect the business and concentrate on running the home and young family; how the growth in our premium income halted and went into decline; how, with so many plates to spin I came close to a breakdown myself; how I seriously considered packing it all in and selling out; how the decline in the growth mysteriously reversed and how I managed to work from home. This was made easier when I discovered at the bottom of our garden, not a fairy exactly, but neighbour Joan Harker who had left her job as PA to a local executive to bring up her children David and Caroline. We came to a neat arrangement by which I handed work over the garden fence and she would pass it back to me completed the following day. Joan proved to be a most valuable secretary to me then and also later when she was appointed Group Personnel Officer.

When I was eventually and gradually able to get back to work after a prolonged absence whilst my wife was out of action, I was a man in a hurry. Perhaps too much so, but there was a lot of catching up to do.

Sat at home I had a lot of time to make plans which, when I got back to work more or less full time, I was itching to put into practice. Plans to fully integrate the two companies, streamline them and take the new organisation forward. Appointments, promotions, staff training, NORMA and marketing my car sticker idea were just a few of the things buzzing though my head. But first there was the Insurance Brokers Registration Act to deal with – an irritation I could well have done without at this particular time. The task ahead of me was enormous and entailed a massive reorganisation of many aspects of the company in order to conform to the requirements of the Act. With the compliance date of 1st December 1981 rapidly approaching and with so many other important things needing my attention I simply couldn't find the quality time to devote to the implementation of the numerous and complex changes to our procedures that would have to be put in place. I needed total peace and quiet and this is where our static caravan in the Lake District came in handy. I packed the car with mountains of paperwork intending to isolate myself for as long as it took to achieve the task. It quickly became apparent that this would be impossible in time for the compliance deadline and that we would therefore, be kicked out of BIBA (The British Insurance Brokers Association). In dismay I began to think about the implications of this and frankly, apart from the fact that we could no longer call ourselves insurance *brokers* I struggled to find any other downside to our failure to register. Why then I asked myself was this legislation introduced in the first place? What was its purpose, I wondered? Presumably to provide some form of consumer protection, but if that were the case then why pick on full-time insurance brokers? We already had high standards of professionalism. Our customers were protected by professional indemnity (errors and omissions) insurance which was not a requisite of other insurance intermediaries. Therefore it would have made sense surely for the legislation to have addressed the mis-selling by all those unprofessional part time agents who sold insurance as a side-line. Instead, estate agents, travel agents, garages, supermarkets, Tom, Dick and Harry were not required to conform to standards laid down by the Act and, incredibly, escaped regulation and its consequences. So, I concluded, there was nothing in it for us and nothing in it for our customers either. Was there something in it perhaps for those officers of BIBA who would sit on the Insurance Brokers Registration Council? Was it a case of jobs for the boys? Were they to be remunerated at the expense of tax payers, Quango fashion, for regulating insurance brokers who didn't need regulating? I wrote to BIBA putting the points to them and asking them to give me a reason why I should register and apart from no longer being able to call myself an insurance *broker* they could offer none. By exposing this glaring and to me, obvious, inadequacy in the legislation, BIBA who had sponsored the Act, would be embarrassed so they asked me not to make public my conclusions. I should have ignored their request and done so but I didn't have the time to embark on this particular crusade for common sense. I needed to devote my time to more pressing personal and corporate matters.

My next priority was to tackle the ULR problem. Uninsured loss recovery was a time consuming unrewarding aspect of the business which caused a lot of hassle. It wasn't really our problem that to save money people would, contrary to our advice and recommendation, take out inadequate cover. For example, they would agree to pay the first £10 or £25 of damage to their car (called an excess) or, instead of taking comprehensive cover, would make do with third party, under which they would have to pay all their own repair costs in full, but for which the premium (and therefore our commission) would be roughly half that of comprehensive cover. Most people are incredibly optimistic when it comes to buying insurance. "It will never happen to me" is the attitude they take. Most resent having to take out insurance at all and probably wouldn't bother if it wasn't compulsory by law. It is an intangible product which people cannot enjoy the immediate visible benefit of and which they just don't need – until they do of course. It was bad enough restricting their cover, paying us a lower premium and reducing our commission too, but what made it particularly irritating was that when they had an accident they expected us to become unpaid solicitors and pursue claims against the drivers of the other vehicles involved. It became pointless trying to explain to clients that it wasn't our fault that they had chosen not to take out fully comprehensive cover. People are not known for their reasonable behaviour when it comes to insurance, particularly so after they have been involved in an accident, which is never their fault of course. They then become even more unreasonable, irrational even, and if the accident was the other driver's fault, downright angry – not however at the driver who had crashed into them. No, their frustration would be taken out on our poor member of staff at the other side of the counter who would be on the receiving end of something like: "What do you mean I will have to go to a solicitor to make a claim against that stupid sod who crashed into me? Why should I have to pay a solicitor when it wasn't my fault? I paid my premium to you and I expect you to sort it out – and if you don't I'll write to the newspapers."

At such times clients were not in their most receptive understanding mood. The last thing they wanted was a lengthy explanation as to why they were not fully covered and how we unsuccessfully tried to persuade them to pay a bit more money to avoid the situation in which they then found themselves. This approach would only inflame the situation and with other customers within earshot these were situations we could do without. Assurances that any solicitors' costs would ultimately be reimbursed by the other driver's insurance company didn't help much. People those days were in awe of solicitors who they felt, rightly or wrongly, were unapproachable – a far cry from the ambulance chasing rabble some of them have become today. So, with no solution to be found in that direction we just had to reconcile ourselves to being frustrated and to handling as best we could our client's uninsured loss claims. But we found a way to make money out of it.

Premises were bought in Monk Street, Sunderland, and a car repair business was set up and customers who wanted us to handle their uninsured loss claims would be required to have their cars repaired there. Wheatsheaf Coachworks had three partners each with an equal share – myself, John Baker a friend of mine in the car repair business and Ian Fletcher. Much of the working capital and all the customers were supplied by Marshall Arnott Ltd. Yes, Ian was well rewarded for what I thought had been his dedication.

It wasn't long before I recognised another business opportunity. With their cars in for repair some customers needed temporary alternative transport. The coachworks had made some profit in its early years and I chose not to draw my share of it. This together with the initial interest free loan of £14,850 made by Marshall Arnott Ltd to fund the purchase of the property, facilitated the purchase of a small fleet of cars available on loan or hire to customers. In cases of non-fault accidents customers would sign a credit hire agreement which meant that they would not need to pay the hire charge until a claim, which included the cost of the car hire, had been successfully concluded by Arnotts against the insurers of the at fault third party driver. This was to my knowledge the first scheme of its kind in the country. It has since been copied and adopted on a large scale and a lot of people have made a lot of money out of my idea. Large national companies have been built on the concept, like Helphire plc who were to feature in my life some twenty years later.

To run the insurance operation in my absence I had appointed Ian Fletcher and Iain Ferguson as directors and had given Ian Fletcher a 10% shareholding. Dave Smith was promoted to North East Motor Underwriting Manager and Dennis Mee replaced him as Middlesbrough branch manager. Scotland was running smoothly in the care of Marilyn, Barbara McGrotty and the two Eileens – Reid and O'Donnell. Other recruits included Les Wood a Fellow of the CII, Robert Newton from our Sunderland rivals Arthur MacBeth Ltd, Terry Henderson another ex V & G man, Ken Lee ACII, Alan Crawford and Gerrard O'Connor.

Les Wood became the manager of our new office in Westgate Road, Newcastle and was replaced by Terry Henderson when Les was promoted to Teesside Regional Manager. Robert Newton, who later became our Group General Manager, was then the Sunderland manager with Ken Lee as his deputy, Alan Crawford as Motor Underwriting Manager and Gerry Robertson (later Burge) and Pat Tiffany on admin. Jan Kennedy looked after the accounts and Gerrard assisted me with our commercial clients.

I was desperate not to lose staff during this particularly vulnerable period and it was a blow when Jan Kennedy handed in her notice but she was persuaded to stay after talking over with her the reasons for leaving. These boiled down to her working hours clashing with her children's school times. Since she was not employed in a client contact role it wasn't necessary for her to keep strictly to office opening hours so I put a proposition to her. Instead of paying her for the number of hours she worked we would agree a "fee" for managing the accounts which she could do at her convenience – in the middle of the night if she chose – as long as the job got done. This suited her perfectly and she remained in that post until she retired. There we were again. Market leaders. Flexi time was introduced into the general work place a decade later. Solutions can be found to most problems given an open mind and a bit of common sense.

I later placed Gerrard O'Connor in charge of our commercial department, a step taken with much reluctance on my part since, apart from the time consuming aspect, I still enjoyed the up-front contact with our commercial clients. The decision was taken in the interest of progress and of course to demonstrate that the boss practices what he preaches by making himself redundant. It wasn't easy to sever my business connections with these clients, many of whom had become friends and were interesting and amusing characters. One of them had told me to insure the contents of his factory – except the clock. "Nobody will steal that," he explained, "My employees watch it constantly." And there was the Jewish businessman who refused to insure against flood. "I don't know how to start a flood," he explained.

No longer able personally to be a hands on manager because of the number of branches to cover and their spread geographically, it was clear to me that a quality and well-motivated workforce was needed to keep us ahead of our competitors, particularly if further expansion was envisaged . It is a reality of business that you can't stand still. You either go forward or you go backward. We must, I knew, devote time and resources to staff recruiting and training and I was well aware that without a career path the resources would not be well spent if our best people simply moved on to find better future prospects elsewhere. My philosophy was that if we had a bright young clerk who had the potential to become a bright young manager then this would allow us to open a new branch to give him or her their opportunity. I would encourage ambitious members of staff to make themselves redundant in their existing jobs, or more accurately their existing duties, by organising their work and by delegation, thus freeing themselves to be considered for promotion. "I don't want you to work hard," I would tell them. "I want you to work effectively, always keeping in mind our objectives." This philosophy can only work in a growing organisation where the threat of job losses doesn't exist and the opportunity for promotion does. Thus, growth would be self-perpetuating. I was so fortunate in those days to be able to recruit and promote my workforce in the way I felt best suited my company's needs and not to satisfy some idiotic piece of legislation. I chose a predominantly female staff because on the whole I considered them better suited to the customer contact side of the business. I promoted them, with one or two exceptions, only when I was suitably reassured that they were unlikely to leave and start a family soon after I'd spent a lot of time and money training them. They respected my frankness and understood my concerns and my honesty in sharing these with them – unlike bosses of today who don't dare do so and have to revert to devious stratagems to avoid prosecution.

Always looking for ways to improve the quality of our workforce we offered, in their placement year, jobs to students taking BA (Hons) degrees at local colleges. It was a good method of staff selection. The students spent a year finding out whether a career in insurance appealed to them and we spent twelve months 'interviewing' them. Several joined us permanently after they had returned to college and qualified. A staff training programme was set up starting with my 'Mr Men' induction course designed to convince newcomers of the importance of the part played by insurance in society and commerce and in which I demonstrated with the aid of Mr Forgetful, Mr Clumsy and Mr Clever the concept of risk management and assessment, the need for an insurance fund and how to ensure that we each contribute a fair share into it. Training was later given on procedures and operation manuals were produced so that each branch would operate in a similar way in order to facilitate staff movement between branches and as cover for sickness and holidays. John Cleese's Video Arts company had produced some excellent training videos and these helped to make our training sessions light-hearted. I had also built up a very good relationship with Bob Campbell, the Underwriter of Lovat Motor Policies at Lloyds, based at Ipswich. Bob too was a keen advocate of proper staff training and like me, was prepared to give up his time for the cause. He organised periodic three day training sessions at the White Hart Hotel in Ipswich for staff from his supporting agents and I was invited to participate by chairing the 'Agent's View' sessions. I used the opportunity to always take along with me two or three of our own members of staff who were thereby able to meet young people from other organisations like ours. These outings were thoroughly enjoyed and most worthwhile. I was very proud of the Arnott delegates who were invariably among the brightest and most confident people there. I couldn't help boasting about them when on one occasion during my session, whilst pontificating on the importance of education, I proudly announced that the three Arnott delegates with me on that occasion, Eileen Reid, Eileen O'Donnell and Barbara McGrotty from Glasgow, had all been to Cambridge. I'm not sure how the other delegates reacted. Some may have been impressed, others may have had their doubts, and not without reason, since our girls were the products of Govan comprehensive and similar institutions. It was only a white lie though. On our way down from the North I had taken a wrong turning and we found ourselves snarled up in the rush hour traffic of the university city of Cambridge!

I had come up with my car sticker idea several years earlier but, in order to maximise its impact, I decided to wait until the company and its client base had grown and was better organised. Our competitors usually followed our marketing lead and were soon into leaflets and Yellow Pages where from being a big fish in a little pool, we were now one of many who had taken half and full page adverts in the car insurance section. We reduced our exposure there and saved money by getting our clients to advertise for us. Each was given a WE ARNOTT INSURED car sticker. To encourage clients to display the stickers we offered them discounts off their next premiums and in some cases a free renewal if their car was lucky enough to be chosen by our roving 'sticker spotters'. To ensure that clients were encouraged to display the stickers and to spread the word, we made sure that lots of cars were 'spotted' and their owners given discount vouchers or free renewals. The scheme proved to be a huge success, with our stickers being seen by probably every motorist, and therefore potential customer, throughout the North East of England, Strathclyde in Scotland and elsewhere.

Another scheme hatched up by my friend Brian Sutherland and I around this time didn't prove to be as successful. Brian Sutherland's venture into his Tudor Garage business after leaving Blue Bell Garages hadn't worked out. We kicked around how best Brian could use his motor trade talents and experience and thus NORMA was born. The Northern Motorists Association again was a first of its kind and attracted the interest of BBC TV. Brian was interviewed on the then popular Nationwide programmed by Frank Bough. I still have the old fashioned video somewhere. The concept was to make available to the growing number of car DIY enthusiasts various goods and services at trade prices. We did this by making all our clients members, which gave NORMA massive buying clout. It was also a back door way of negotiating a discounted insurance scheme for NORMA members – in effect Arnott clients. The weakness of the scheme was that whilst benefiting Arnotts and their clients and the suppliers, who were now selling lots of goods for cash, it did not itself generate any income. Various attempts were made to rectify this but the suppliers didn't respond when we asked them to check the identity of our members who, we discovered, were lending their cards to all and sundry. Nor did our clients take kindly to the suggestion that they paid a small fee for membership. Had we devoted more time to NORMA I'm sure we would have come up with a way forward but I felt that we could find a better use for Brian's talents in another direction. The NORMA office was closed and Brian joined the Arnott team at Middlesbrough where his motor sales experience brought a refreshing new dimension to our approach to new business. Our marketing and our reputation ensured that we stimulated a lot of enquiries but our conversion or 'strike' ratio could, we felt, be improved. Brian was engaged in an up-front sales and training capacity dealing with prospective new customers, a role in which he was well suited. His approach to the sale manifested itself instantly with a dramatic improvement in our new business figures and it was so simple. Having given a quote to a customer Brian would enquire how this compared with the customer's existing insurer's renewal premium or with other quotes he had received. It usually compared favourably whereupon Brian would start filling in a proposal form. Faced with a virtual *fait accomplis* most of them just went along with it, paid their money and left the office clutching a cover note and a receipt for their premium. Those who did find the courage to suggest that they wanted time to think about it were greeted by Brian's standard reaction – a puzzled expression and the question "What is there to think about? I'm giving you a better policy at a cheaper price and you will be dealing with the region's major car insurance provider?" followed immediately by the next question on the proposal form. Few escaped his clutches. We incorporated this example of 'closing the sale' into our staff training and linked our staff bonus scheme to 'strike rate'. In those branches where Brian's approach was adopted the percentage of enquiries converted into clients improved dramatically and the staff enjoyed healthy increases in their bonuses. Brian was later to find his niche in another area of insurance in which he made a very successful career.

Things were going well in the nineteen eighties, but two things happened in that decade which conspired to eventually change all that. I joined Lloyds as an underwriting 'Name' and I met Brooks Mileson.

**With Gerrard O'Connor, winner of the first Arnott Masters
Golf jacket, 1990.**

Seven

WE ARNOTT AMUSED

*I consider neither vehicle was to blame but, if either
vehicle was to blame, it was the other one.*
A claimant

IN ONE OF THE ISSUES of our PR publication *Arnott News*, an
extract from which is appended, I included some extracts from
claim forms completed by clients who had been involved in accidents.
This stimulated a lot of interest from a number of Insurance
Companies and Lloyds Motor Syndicates, some of whom, I learned,
kept 'funny files' too. The outcome was a lively exchange of material
between us all, from which I built up a substantial dossier of
interesting and amusing accounts of real incidents and situations. I
have selected some of my favourite tales of woe and reproduced them
more or less verbatim. I hope you find them as entertaining as we did.

Acknowledgements to Mike Warner of Hartley Cooper and Warner,
Colin Armstrong of Corinthian Motor Policies, Gillian from HR
Wilson & Partners, Marilyn Thomson from our Glasgow Office, Julie
and Janie from Middlesbrough and to everyone who has contributed to
my funny file.

BIRD PARTY – Mrs E.Z, 1989

"I was driving up Mallowdale, Nunthorpe at about 25 mph. The bird
slipped under the car leaving a cloud of feathers behind me. I stopped
the car to check the bird, noticing its stomach had fallen out. I
checked the pulse. None. I knew it was a waste of time giving it the

kiss of life. I placed it on the grass, and on the way back collected it. It all happened so fast I didn't get a chance to brake. I thought the bird was flying over but it swooped."

Mrs Z brought her claim form into the office accompanied by a shoe box which contained the remains of the "third party".

OH SHIT – Mr J.N. 1984

At exit to car park the Escort halted. The driver of the Mazda tried to stop behind but her foot slipped off the brake pedal (she had unknowingly stood on dog dirt and it was on the sole of her shoe). Cause of accident – driver error/dirty dog.

BOBBIES WILL BE BOBBIES – Mr P.R. 1986

"My Land Rover was parked on Seaton front with other Land Rovers. He noticed my tax disc had just run out. So he told me to get into the back seat of his car. So I did. He reversed up to me and stayed right next to me and that's how we had the crash cos when I got back into the Land Rover I moved my dog over and then I went to put my seat belt on and I heard the Bobby car start. There was a big bang. Then they sat in his car for a couple of minutes. Then he got out and said "Look what you've done now" and I said "I've done nowt you forgot to take your car out of reverse didn't you?" and he said "Get out" so I did and he said "What's your handbrake doing off?" and I said "I never even had my keys in the Land Rover". I was in his car for a good twenty minutes and the Land Rover never shook or anything. It stood solid as a rock. But they are trying to blame me. Who in their right mind would run into the back of a police car? I'm only me and a bobby is a bobby. So when the other bobby came along he started taking photos. Then he asked me what was wrong are you cold cos I was shaking and I said no. I am just shocked at the way these two are going on. So I got in he's car and I asked him if he would take me to the police station cos I'm saying nothing where those two are, and he said he couldn't. So I told him that they were blaming me, but I don't think he believed me, but a lad walked past and an officer said something to him and he kept on walking and came home, and sold the Land Rover the same day and that is the truth."

CAR PARK RAGE – Mrs S, 1992

The following is a graphic description of the animosity between the parties involved which left us completely in the dark as to what actually happened between the vehicles involved.

"I drove my car JEF xxx to park the car in car park at the rear of Albert Road, I drove the car passed the space behind my car which was clear. I drove forward and then reversed into car space as there didn't seem to be a lot of room in the space I choose to use, I drove away and drove over the other side of the car park where no cars were parked at all, my daughter got out to pay fee of 15 p and she said this lady and sons were shouting what I'd done to her car. I went over and try to reason with her, she said I wasn't fit to drive, the elder son called my daughter a tramp. She said if she was tramp, he was a creep. I asked the lady driving to stay where she was till the police was brought it. She went hysterical. I tried to reason with her saying details were to be taken. All she said was to her son take this woman's number (crossed out) fucking number. I asked her not to drive away for the police to see how she was parked and also to sort something out. As I went to the car the elder boy (about 16) hit my right arm and hand which they noticed had a bandage on. I then spoke to the lady seated in the car and she closed the car on my left hand trapping my fingers and thumb and she proceeded to park the car in a different part of the car park. She said if I prosecuted her in any way I would suffer and shouted nothing but abuse. After this report, in intend going to the General Hospital as I feel all shook up and both hands are aching.

I went to police station they advised me to go to get number off Swansea for small fee, also as far as they were concerned on a public car park this incident is a common assault either to do it myself or consult a solicitor."

ALWAYS LOCK IN YOUR MIRROW – Mr A.C, 1987

"I WAS DRIVING ALONG WINTERBOTTOM AVENU SLOWING DOWN TO TURN WRIGHT. LOCKED IN MY DOOR MIRROW TO SEA IF ENEYTHING WOS BEHIND ME SEEN NOTHING WENT TO INDICAT RIGHT AND BANG LOCKED RIGHT AND SORE A RED CAR DRIVING PAST ME TRAVELING BETWEEN 35 TO 45 MPH TO MY ESTIMATE. I THEN TURNED RIGHT AGROSS THE WITE LINE TO THE HOTHER SIDE OF THE ROAD INTO BRUCE CRESANT AND STOPPED MY VAN AND GOT OUT LOCKED AT THE PONT OF IMPACT ON MY VAN AND SORE A SCRAP ON MY FRONT BUMPER. LOCKED UP THE ROAD TO SEA IF THE RED CAR HAD STOPED AND SORE 3 LADIES STANDING TO 150 YARDS UP THE ROAD ONE OF THEM SHOUTED COME HEAR YOU BASTERD. SO I GOT IN MY VAN AND WENT UP TO THEM AND STOPED BEHIND THEM GOT OUT APOLIGISED AND LOCKED AT THE DAMAGE TO THE CAR WICHE WOS A DEEP SCRA FROM THE WEELARCH ON THE BACK OF THE CAR ABOOT 8.16 INCHES LONG, ONE OF THE LADIES SED TO ME YOU DID NOT INDICATE AND WE THORTE YOU WERE STOPPING. BUT I HAD NOT STARTED TO TURN UNTIL AFTER THE IMPACT AND THE RED CAR HAD GONE PAST ME. THE REASON I DID NOT SEA THE RED CAR IN MY MIRROW WHEN I LOCKED WAS IT WAS OVER THE WITE LINE ON THE HOTHER SIDE OF THE ROAD AT THE TIME I LOCKED IN MY MIRROW AND IT MUST HAVE BEEN HARFE WAY PAST ME OUT OF VIEW OF MY MIRROW."

HEAD FOR DISASTER. Mr R.T, 1987

"Gary J Lane asked for me to take him out on my girlfriend's motorcycle. I did not want to go but he put petrol into the bike. He took me along a road I had never been along before and whilst travelling he tapped me on the shoulder to attract my attention. Then he turned my head round so he could talk to me. When I turned back there was a right hand bend. I realised I couldn't get round so kept the bike straight, braked and slowed right down. Ran out of road and we both fell off on to a grass bank.

Mr G.J. Lane has admitted to police in writing that he was to blame."

FREEWHEELING – Mr W.S. 1990

"I turned into Bevington Road from Trinity Road and was face with a car zig zagging across the road completely out of control. The driver of this car was hanging on to the outside of the car trying to grab the steering wheel. Having failed to hold the car back he abandoned the vehicle, the car gathered speed, careered across the road with the driver running behind. At the time of impact the driver was some distance away."

WHOA THERE, Mr P.L. 1982

"I saw a horse charging down the road towards me, I drove to the offside to try to avoid the horse, but the horse went to the offside as well. I then drove back to the nearside and the horse still came charging at the motor. I slowed the car down and proceeded to get as close as possible to the kerb. By this time the vehicle was stationary but the horse kept on running at the car. I realised it wasn't going to stop and I pushed myself over the back seat. As I was scrambling over, the horse collided feet and head first into the Mini."

A BAD SIGN – Mr L.S. 1978

"I saw two vehicles had hit the rear end of my car and had rammed it into a road sign that said 'Good Driving Saves Lives'."

THE TRICLOPTIC CLAIMANT – Mr J.R. 1984

"I had one eye on a parked car, another eye on approaching lorries and another on the woman behind."

CHICKEN – From a witness

"I am PC X stationed at St George. I was on patrol in Lodge Causeway where I saw a Mk III Cortina and a Triumph 2000 motor car travelling at speeds, I would estimate in excess of 60 mph, along Lodge Causeway. I signalled the vehicles to stop by flashing my torch and giving a number one stop signal. Both vehicles failed to slow down and changed direction, driving straight at me. I took evasive action, i.e. 'jumped out of the bloody way'."

WOBBLY WRITING – From an injured third party

"I was given heat treatment and exercises. I have notified my GP that I am having pains during sexual intercourse and am still having pain at this moment whilst writing this letter."!!!

THE GYMNAST – Mr H, 1977

"I looked in my mirror, indicated and pulled towards the centre of the road to turn right into Francis Rd. As I was making the turn which was on black ice a motor cyclist which was travelling uphill from Stitchley hit me and was thrown onto the bonnet sliding over coming to rest on my offside standing on his feet."

PLAYFUL PUSSY – From a Personal Accident Claimant

"I always sleep in a shirt, nothing else, and on the morning of the 17th February I went downstairs to get a drink. As I reached down to get it out of the fridge our ten week old kitten thought I was playing with it and jumped up from behind digging its claws into my exposed dangly bits from which it remained suspended until I could prize its claws free"

Ouch!

THE RABBIT & THE SNAKE – *A defence by the third party to a claim against her, made on behalf of our client. It was accompanied by four detailed diagrams.*

Diagram 1.	Wife driving.	Me "Darling you are going the wrong way my sweet" (BOWDLERISED conversation) – look it up. We did – it means censored. STOPS (stop lights come on)
Diagram 2.		Engages reverse gear and REVERSE LIGHTS COME ON.
Diagram 3.		Reverses.
Diagram 4.		Result – a bump.

At no time did your client hoot, shout, or reverse and hoot which I think he should have done, just sat there like a rabbit in front of a snake.

P.S. Married 39 years.

MITIGATON GALORE – Mr D.W. 1978

Even after all these years it never ceases to amaze me what extraordinary lengths some motorists will go to in order to protest their innocence. Despite Mr W's endeavours Mrs C was paid compensation and Mr W lost his no claims bonus.

I was travelling eastwards on the A 28 in Wincheap, Canterbury, and saw Mrs C stationary on the centre island, waiting to cross. She gave me the impression that she would prefer to wait. I proceeded but then the very bright sun at low elevation suddenly shone through a row of chimneys, or a reflection from a stationary or moving object, blinded me.

My sun visor was in the down position. I normally move to the right of the driver's seat, as the visor covers the centre rear mirror. This enables me to take advantage of the off-side wing mirror.

In this driving position the off-side windscreen post creates a blind spot.

The combination of these factors were responsible for my not seeing Mrs C, who changed her mind and decided to cross at the crossing.

The location of the accident, to a stranger to Canterbury, is noted for the number of distractions which are listed below.

1. Windows and signs with reflective surfaces to divert powerful direct sunlight, which existed at the time of the accident. The London temperature that day rose to 77 degrees Fahrenheit (reported on front page of Daily Express 12/10/78)
2. A "Roundabout Ahead" sign.
3. A sign, at two different angles, at the end of the staggered white line, east of the crossing, stating "130 yards."
4. At a different angle "LOW BRIDGE"
5. These are followed by two "End of Speed Limit" signs, on each side of the road.
6. These are followed by a Roundabout Direction sign.
7. Then the unusual (to a visitor) light strip across the road (the Railway Bridge) which is an alarming sight to myself, a stranger.

Furthermore there are commercial projecting signs, which have to be visually checked, in order to verify their status.

The combination of the above, coupled with the fact that, as a stranger to Canterbury, driving in a queue of commuters, who know the city intimately, I was conscious of creating delaying tactics, in comparison to residents, who unconsciously know of the presence and meaning of the driver aid signs.

Adversely, due to parked cars adjacent to the island, my car was positioned near to the island, so minimising my chances, should a pedestrian suddenly decide to step off the island, as in this case.

During the statement submitted to the police station, I was informed that they had experienced trouble at that particular crossing previously.

After the accident in an attempt to locate Mrs C's husband, I spoke to a housewife neighbour who quoted "Mrs. C does move very quickly." When I revealed that she had been involved in an accident she replied "Oh, not another accident."

I am so eager to prove the adverse conditions created by the brilliant sunshine, that I have contacted the University of London Observatory, regarding the elevation of the sun at 08.40 hours on the 11/10/78.

They have furnished the following – 12 degrees above the horizon at a compass bearing of 117 degrees East from North

With the aid of a sextant, I intend to take a bearing at the scene of the accident, to verify the contribution made by strong sunlight, to this accident.

HERD THIS ONE? – Mr B T, 1994

Whilst travelling from A to B on a minor road in N Cornwall we stopped for a herd of cows. The field gates had been opened by a Welsh Collie! The herd, of Friesian variety, consisted of about 100 cattle. An evil eyed beast some 20 feet away obviously decided to lash out at the nearest object on passing. The car was dented on the off side over the front wheel arch. No communication was made as I cannot bark in Welsh or moo in Dutch. The only temporary mishap which occurred was washed off on our return to the hotel.

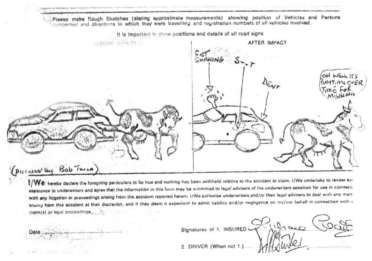

One of the more descriptive and artistic sketches from the funny file.

NOW SOME ONE LINERS

The definitive list (so far) of those classic claim form comments.

Driver leaned forward to swat a fly on the windscreen and hit the car in front.

Coming home I drove into the wrong house and collided with a tree I don't have.

The other car collided with mine without giving warning of its intentions.

I thought my window was down, but I found out it was up when I put my hand through it.

I collided with a stationary truck coming the other way.

A truck backed through my windshield into my wife's face.

A pedestrian hit me and went under my car.

The guy was all over the road. I had to swerve a number of times before I hit him.

I pulled away from the side of the road, glanced at my mother-in-law and headed over the embankment.

In an attempt to kill a fly, I drove into a telephone pole.

I had been shopping for plants all day and was on my way home. As I reached an intersection a hedge sprang up, obscuring my vision and I did not see the other car.

I had been driving for 40 years when I fell asleep at the wheel and had an accident.

I was on my way to the doctor with rear end trouble when my universal joint gave way causing me to have an accident.

As I approached the intersection a sign suddenly appeared in a place where no stop sign had ever appeared before. I was unable to stop in time to avoid the accident.

To avoid hitting the bumper of the car in front I struck the pedestrian.

My car was legally parked as it backed into the other vehicle.

An invisible car came out of nowhere, struck my car and vanished.

I told the police I was not injured, but on removing my hat found that I had a fractured skull.

I was sure the old fellow would never make it to the other side of the road when I struck him.

The pedestrian had no idea which direction to run, so I ran over him.

I saw a slow moving sad faced old gentleman as he bounced off the roof of my car.

The indirect cause of the accident was a little guy in a small car with a big mouth.

I was thrown from my car as it left the road. I was later found in a ditch by some stray cows.

I knocked over the man, he admitted it was his fault as he had been knocked over before.

Dog on the road applied brakes, causing a skid.

I left my car unattended for a few minutes and whether by accident or design it ran away.

I was scraping my rearside on a bank when the accident happened.

I collided with a stationary tramcar which was coming in the opposite direction.

Coming back, I took the wrong turning and drove into a tree that was not there.

There was no damage to the vehicle, as the gate-post will testify.

I was keeping two yards from each lamp-post, which were in a straight line, unfortunately there was a bend in the road bringing a right-hand lamp-post in line with the others and of course I landed in the river.

To avoid a collision I ran into the other lorry.

I blew my horn, but it had been stolen, and would not work.

A bull was standing near and a bee must have tickled him as he gored my car.

If the other driver had stopped a few yards behind himself nothing would have happened.

Three women were all talking to each other and when two stepped back and one stepped forward I had to have an accident.

Whilst waiting at traffic lights I was rammed by the stationary car behind me.

I was having a dispute with my wife, she pulled my hair causing me to turn into a lamp standard.

I did not take the name of the witness as in their ignorance they said I was to blame.

I sounded my horn, the pedestrian ran for the pavement, but I got him.

One wheel went into the ditch, my foot jumped from the brake to the accelerator pedal, leapt across to the other side and jammed into the trunk of a tree.

My boots must have made me drive faster than intended, although I was not exceeding the speed limit

AND ONE FROM THE USA

"This is what can happen when people don't think things through," Lt James McDonagh of the Calhoun County Sheriff's Department told a press conference in Michigan. "The driver got lost this morning in the Leroy township area, and when he backed into a field to turn around near J Drive South, his Mercury sedan became stuck in the mud. After several futile attempts to free his car, with his rear wheels just spinning around, he suddenly thought of a way to get the vehicle out of the mud. But in retrospect, he can see now that it wasn't a very bright idea.

"He placed his toolbox on the accelerator to rev the engine, then got behind the car, and tried to push it free. He was successful in freeing the vehicle, but hadn't thought about how he would then regain control of it. Once it was out of the mud, the Mercury sedan accelerated across a cut soybean field, killing a cow in the process, while the man ran helplessly behind. It travelled half a mile, reaching an estimated speed of 100 mph and sometimes becoming airborne, before crashing into a tree. The impact crushed the car back to the windshield, which is how we could estimate the speed. No tickets were issued, and we won't be releasing the driver's name. He's suffered enough already." *(Battle Creek Enquirer,* 29/12/05.)

THE HOT SEAT

A claims negotiator's job can be scary as the following extract from a report on a claim against Corinthian Motor Policies at Lloyds demonstrates. The investigator survived.

"On the 27th November I had an eventful meeting at the third party's home. For the record and because there could be a possibility of the family difficulties causing stress to the third party which she is blaming upon the accident I relate the situation that developed whilst I was in the house.

I arrived as arranged at the home at 12 o'clock and was invited into the lounge by Mrs X. She is of foreign origin but clearly has been in this country for many years. I gather her husband works as a Farm Manager and the house is owned by the Estate but is detached and was very well furnished. I was invited to sit down and asked whether I would like a coffee. I was happy to accept this. Whilst Mrs X was in the kitchen I heard the front door open and into the lounge walked a youth of approximately 23 years of age wearing a woollen hat, dark glasses and a long overcoat. He immediately challenged me by asking what I was doing in the house and as this I felt did not deserve a reply I ignored it but he in a threatening manner asked again and I explained why I was there. He went out of the room and Mrs X came back in, in a somewhat tearful state, explaining that her Son was a little odd. She went out of the room again and in marched the man again shouting to me that he could not understand why strangers always came into the house, he hated strangers and could not stand their presence. He marched out again. I deduced that this man was a little odd and ought to be watched but at this stage was not unduly worried. The mother came back into the room and said that as her husband had not turned up she would telephone to see whether he had forgotten the appointment and this she did. Immediately the youth came back into the lounge and with a clenched fist held this against my jaw and demanded that I vacated the chair in a somewhat threatening manner. He only needed to ask me twice and I quickly obliged. I thought at this stage that he would sit in the chair and that my best course was to seek the company of the mother by the telephone. I accordingly walked to the hall where Mrs X was gaily talking to her husband totally ignoring my peril. As I walked to the door the youth stayed with me with his fist now up against my left jaw and shouting as we moved across the lounge to get out of the house. I was at this stage becoming just a little concerned as to my well-being and in a stronger voice as possible asked Mrs X whether I was safe. Her reaction was to tell the man to leave the room. She merely said that he had not hit anyone yet.

I decided that it would be just as well to stay and endeavour to discuss the claim and accordingly I sat back into the chair. The young man sat in the sofa and started to criticise the various articles of clothing that he was wearing. The mother was somewhat tearful and I was grateful to hear the arrival of the father. He had a short spell talking to the wife and I was somewhat surprised that he made no comment whatever about my predicament. I felt it was perhaps not too wise to raise the issue as it might well have been all a dream. We then discussed the claim and the youth from time to time chimed in but one or other of the parents told him to shut up."

NEVER NEVER

To pay claims we've got to collect the premiums which can sometimes be a painstaking process. To finish this Chapter I have reproduced a series of letters From Mrs H, one of our Glasgow clients. We would have had to have hearts of stone to ignore her pleas for extended credit.

"Dear Arnot Notheren,

I am writing to you on behalf of my husband he was paid off his work about 5 weeks ago as I told you when I phoned you and I asked you to let me pay my husband 3 payment of his insurance in two parts well my husband has been waiting to be payed by the unemployment office but has not received any thing yet so please will you help me out I want to pay it and keep my insurance with you it will never happen again as my husband is waiting to here from a job I will either pay it all this week or half this week and the rest the following week if that is all write with you I will definetly pay it this time please help as wee need the can as my little boy of 2 is not well and we have to take him to the hospital so please help.

Yours faithfully

Mrs H"

"Dear Sir or Madam,

I wrote to you about two weeks ago about my husband Insurance with you, and you let me pay it at a later date which is due on the 15th June, well first I want to thank you very much for extending it for me and to let you know my situation now I am very embarrast telling you this and hope that you understand my situation. I know that it is due and I was sending it when I got a letter from my electric board and I have been put off of the scheme I was on and have to pay my full amount in my bill which is £124.00 or they will disconnect me I am very embarrest at what has come of all this all because of my husband pay off at work I hope you understand as I don't I have never been in this situation in my life as you will know I have always paid you on time so if you could just let me have another week to pay I will scrape up the money and send the full payment next week I hope everything I have told you is in confidence and again hope you can help me as I am crying out for it.

Yours faithfully,

Mrs H"

"Dear Arnott Insurance,

I wrote to you on behafe of my husbands car insurance with you you have very kindly gave me more time to pay it and I am realy greatfull to you I cannot phone you because I got my phone changed and I cannot phone out only incoming calls because I cannot afford it so please he has not been using the car until he had the rest of the money to let you understand could you live on £62 per fortnight well we cannot the D.H.S. are still trying to see if we are due any more money but I have got someone in the house and do not know how much I owe you please I am so sorry for all the trouble I have caused so if you let me know I will send it to you as soon as possible when I receve your letter or if you want to phone me please help me.

Yours faithfully,

Mrs H"

"Dear Arnot Notheren,

I am writing to you on behalf of my husbands car Insurance with you, well to let you know what has been happening and hope that you understand you have been very kind and have gave me a bit of time to pay it and I am very thankfull to you I am very sorry I am late in paying the payment due to you well to let you know ever since my husband has lost his job everything has gone wrong with us you see my husband did not get any redindance pay or holiday pay when he was payed off and we are having a bit of trouble with my husbands money he was due his unemployment benefit two weeks ago and has still not received anything yet I have been phoneing them and they say that there is something wrong with his claim and that it will take a little time to come through we have been living with my mother because of this we do not have the money to keep my house going because of this situation I am in. What is worrying me is that I will send you all the money I have got and if you could please let me have just a little more time to pay the rest I can assure you this would not have happened if we were getting our money on time I would have paided it weeks ago, my husband will not be using the car until I have payed the rest you see I could just not pay the rest and I would lose the money I have all ready payed and I do not want to do that as I need the car so please could you see your way to letting me have a little more time if not I will try and get the money from somewhere before I would lose my claim so again I thankyou very much for the time you have taken with me.

Yours faithfully,

Mrs H"

"Dear Arnot Notheren,

I am so sorry for the delay in sending you the rest of my money you see I have had a bit of an upset in my family my little boy of 10 month fell and split his head open and had to get 7 stitches so I have not been with myself if you could please let me know how much I have still to pay I will send it as I have forgotten again I am sorry and thank you very much for your help.

Yours faithfully,

Mrs H"

Well Mrs H, I hope your little boy recovered from his misfortunes and has grown up into a healthy young man and I hope Mr H managed to find employment, your electric bill is up to date and you are both well.

Eight

A SMALL FORTUNE AT LLOYDS

Getting a bit wet under the collar are we?
Chrissarism

COFFEE WAS INTRODUCED into England in the seventeenth century and quickly became hugely popular, spawning a profusion of coffee houses in London. Some fifty years after the first record of the existence of coffee in England, Edward Lloyd in 1687 opened his coffee house in the docklands area of the city. It soon became very popular with ships' captains and crews who would meet there to exchange information on maritime routes and conditions. It also attracted merchants seeking to negotiate agreements on prices and terms which would include certain guarantees and bonds regarding the safe delivery of their cargoes. The merchant would entrust his cargo to the ship owner who gave the best guarantee, often secured by a charge on the vessel itself, which of course would be worthless if both cargo and ship were to perish. This was an unsatisfactory situation which the ship owners and captains were not at ease with. It wasn't long before a number of individuals, in return for a 'premium' offered to remove the risk from the owners and assume it themselves. They would draw up the terms of the agreement on a slip of paper and each guarantor would sign his name below. These individuals became known as underwriters and in 1771 seventy of them put up one hundred pounds each (a lot of money then) and formed the Society of Lloyds, later to become the Corporation of Lloyds, which in turn became the world's most famous insurance market. Such was the integrity and trust within the market, that huge sums were underwritten, often on a handshake, even before the risk was assessed and a premium agreed, thereby enabling cargoes to be quickly despatched to their destinations across the world.

Lloyds became a household name and the phrase "A1 at Lloyds" was used to describe anything that was of cast iron safety and trustworthiness. It was no surprise therefore that when wealth became more widely spread among us, becoming a Lloyds Underwriter – or Name as they were called – seemed an attractive proposition. It was a way to make money work twice by earning interest or dividends from investments whilst at the same time pledging it to cover insurance losses which for three hundred years had always been more than adequately compensated for by underwriting profits. By virtue of the Lloyds Acts of 1871 and 1911 any losses were allowed against the Names' personal tax and better still, any investment income from the syndicate reserves were distributed to the Names tax-free. This made Lloyds an even more attractive proposition, not only for the traditionally wealthy but also for the new class of high earners in sport, entertainment and business.

During the early left wing 'Robin Hood' Labour government, tax levels reached ninety-eight pence in the pound, which caused an inevitable brain drain as many hard working talented people left the country to earn their living abroad. My own popular GP, Doctor Miller, whose surgery was always packed, was one of many who became disillusioned and emigrated to the USA. Why do these overzealous politicians never stop to consider the obvious consequences of their emotional decisions? Perhaps they lack the intelligence to do so.

There was a reaction from the commercial world to the government's draconian 'solution' to wealth redistribution. Money was moved offshore with ramifications later to the detriment of the country. Devious but legal means were found by Lloyds to create losses for which Names could reclaim 98% from the government, and at the same time to bump up capital appreciation payments which they received tax-free. Instead of raising more money in tax, this ill-conceived government measure, like so many others, had the opposite effect.

Small fortunes were made during Lloyds' halcyon days before the nineteen-eighties when it numbered among its members many famous celebrities, some of whom I was later privileged to meet and share shoulders to cry on. Henry Cooper the boxer, Lester Piggott the jockey, Virginia Wade our ladies Wimbledon champion, Dennis Compton the cricketer and many other people all successful in their own field.

Between 1971 and 1988 membership of Lloyds grew from 6,000 to a peak of 32,433 including 3,400 from the United States and it wasn't only for financial reasons that I myself joined on the 1st January 1980. I was in the insurance business and by then we had developed a strong connection with Lloyds, particularly the motor syndicates, some of whose underwriters I had got to know very well. My status as a Name gave me credibility and enabled me to persuade them to offer Arnotts preferential terms and competitive premiums. But perhaps the fundamental stimulus was the hunger within—the desire to demonstrate to myself and the world that a shy working class kid from a council house estate, once described by the Mayor of Middlesbrough as "A last chance saloon", could aspire to such an exclusive club. I think there is a need to show off within us all.

Daughter Liz was living in London at the time and I was eager to show her the inner sanctum of the famous Lloyds building in Lime Street and have lunch there. Disappointingly we weren't allowed in because she was wearing jeans. What a pity I wasn't annoyed enough to resign my membership there and then.

A Name was required to demonstrate his wealth in readily realisable assets and pledge it to Lloyds to cover losses and to place a bank guarantee or cash deposit of 50% of premiums written. I initially wrote £50,000 in premium which was the minimum allowed. I had mentioned my plans to join Lloyds to my client and friend Joe Laidler and he too became a member on the same day with another Sunderland lad, Les Brown. Prior to the big day we had to undergo an interview in front of the Chairman and Committee of that august institution in the magnificent board room within the even more impressive Lloyds building, after which we were given a conducted tour of the underwriting room crammed with tiny 'boxes' from which the underwriters conducted their business. We were shown the famous Lutine Bell, which was sounded each time there was a maritime disaster, and the fascinating Lloyds museum, followed by lunch in the members only Captains Room. A proud day.

Earlier in the year we had visited Lloyds to meet some of the underwriters who had been selected for us. There had recently been two major air disasters, a runway collision in Tenerife between two Boeing 747s, which killed 583 people, and a crash only a mile from the runway in Chicago after an engine fell off a DC10 claiming 273 lives. I expected our Aviation Underwriter Barry Bowen (Syndicate 862) to have a long face and said as much to him. "Not at all," he replied. "We needed something like that to scare off the non-Lloyds competition and to harden the rates." In hindsight I think perhaps he may have been putting on a brave face to impress us. On a £10,000 line Mr Bowen the following year managed to lose me over £17,000.

We had joined Lloyds through the management agency of David Holman who, shortly after we became "Names", invited us to his annual Names Dinner at the Cavalry & Guards Club in Park Lane at which each Name would be seated between two underwriters who, between each course, would get up and move a couple of places round the table, giving us an opportunity to talk to several different underwriters. I felt distinctly uncomfortable all evening. I had travelled down to London with Joe and Les wearing casual clothes with my best bib and tucker neatly folded away in my suitcase. We booked into our hotel, had a couple of drinks and went to our rooms to get changed, having arranged to meet later in the bar to get a taxi to Park Lane. When I walked into the bar wearing my dinner jacket and black tie I was horrified to see Joe and Les wearing lounge suits. Since I had organised the trip I felt really bad about not mentioning to them to wear dinner jacket and black tie and about how embarrassing it would be for them being the odd ones out – especially on such a grand and important occasion. I wondered why they were amused. "It says lounge suits on our tickets," they said, and sure enough it did. It wasn't the first time and certainly not the last time that with so many things on my mind I hadn't concentrated on detail and acted on assumptions. It was I, not Joe and Les, who was severely embarrassed that evening seated among the Saville Row suits in an old sports jacket, casual shirt and gaudy tie borrowed from reception.

But I was in for an even more embarrassing experience the following morning. I always sleep in my birthday suit and was woken by a loud knock on my bedroom door. Half asleep and fuzzy from an overdose of expensive wine from the night before, I dragged myself out of bed, trudged across and opened the door – or should I say tried to open it. Puzzled and bemused I pushed harder, heard a loud crash and almost fell over as the door suddenly gave way and flew open. I gingerly leaned out pushing the door open a little wider and noticed a bed and mattress in the corridor. There was another bed base leaning against my door poised ready to topple over. As I reached out in vain to stop it my room door clattered shut behind me and left me standing bollock naked in the hotel corridor surrounded by sundry items of furniture, mattresses, brooms, buckets and other cleaning items. The door of the room opposite opened and I saw the black face of its occupant change from perplexity to amusement. But I wasn't able to share his amusement – especially when he called for his female companion to come and have a look. He and she were not the only ones to find my predicament amusing. I could hear raucous Wearside laughter from an alcove a little way down the corridor. A chambermaid then called for the housekeeper who, despite my protestations that I wasn't responsible for the mayhem, gave me a stern ticking off before allowing me back into the sanctuary of my room. To this day Joe reckons that this was the funniest spectacle of his full and fascinating life.

David Holman, our members' agent, had sensibly stressed how important it was to spread our underwriting portfolio across a range of syndicates writing different classes of risk – Marine, Non Marine, Liability, Motor and Aviation – but I wasn't entirely happy that he had placed three new Names on a new Aviation syndicate with no reserves and which had made a heavy loss in its first year, so when I increased my underwriting to £200,000 in 1984 I used another agent John Poland for the other half of my exposure, even though my second and subsequent years of underwriting had produced reasonable profits. At least I would get to enjoy another Names dinner, determined this time to be properly dressed for the occasion!

In 1987 however there was a sharp deterioration in the performance of our syndicates. I was called upon to pay in advance an interim cash call of £18,750 towards losses made by Syndicate 540 managed by the Feltrim agency. The Underwriter of 540, appropriately named Fagan, continued to pick the pockets of his Names big time. This was bad enough but when our other syndicates followed suit alarm bells began to ring. Dark clouds were gathering over Lloyds. The next major syndicate to announce massive losses was managed by the Gooda Walker agency and within a very short space of time every one of our syndicates was posting disastrous losses. By 1992 Lloyds, globally, had lost its Names a staggering £8 billion, an average of £350,000 for each Name.

Now insurance, like bookmaking, isn't rocket science. Bookies very rarely lose money. Sensibly they lay off any heavy bets. Similarly insurers lay off, or reinsure, liabilities in excess of what they can themselves carry comfortably. This finely tuned practice had existed in Lloyds for over three hundred years, so it was quite obvious that something had gone wrong. I won't go into boring detail but the courts were later to describe us Names as innocent victims of staggering incompetence and dishonesty after a previous Chairman had deliberately lied in court. The judge stopped short of mentioning fraud – just. The UK Government did not escape criticism either, since for some unknown and very questionable reasons, it chose to exclude

Lloyds from regulation to protect investors under the Financial Services Act. Why? We are now pretty sure that two major causes of the problems were the Spiral and Asbestos. The Spiral was a system whereby brokers and underwriters conspired to over reinsure, taking a commission from every reinsurance transaction until there was hardly any premium left to pay claims. Syndicates would take on various reinsurance levels of the same risks, not once but several times as it was hawked by the broker 'pass the parcel' style round the market. The underwriter would presumably take a clandestine cut of the broker's commission. They made a lot of easy money at the expense of the Names who were left holding the risk parcel when the music stopped, often with as little as 10% of the original premium left in the pot to pay claims. The second and more serious matter was the asbestosis scandal. This was a time bomb waiting to explode. I must be careful what I say here but I just cannot believe that the experts and insiders at Lloyds were not aware of this long tail liability in the 1970's and 1980's. They certainly did not disclose their fears to Names. Nor did they record them, as they are required to do, in their annual reports. Nor was it made known to us, probably deliberately concealed from us in fact, that our syndicates were taking on types of renegade risks probably asbestos related under reinsurance agreements, thus making a nonsense of the risk spreading concept. No longer could we rely on our Aviation underwriter only insuring aircraft related losses or our Marine underwriter only covering maritime risks, etc. etc. Were we being deliberately and surreptitiously exposed to the looming avalanche of USA asbestos claims? Was the reason for the heavy recruitment of Names in the 1980's to get more rich guys and girls into the fold to pay the impending losses? One well-intentioned Name actually bought his poor wife a Lloyds membership for her birthday! Joe also persuaded Dorothy his wife to join, the consequences of which were still being felt twenty-five years later. Recruit to dilute was the charge levelled at Lloyds. The cost in wealth and hardship was only part of the tragic story of Lloyds treachery. There were several suicides, including the young man assigned by

David Holman to deal with our affairs, John Matson, who wasn't a wealthy man and who presumably had put up his home as surety.

Wealth is rarely created by entering lotteries or filling in football coupons. It is created by clever hard working people – people who do not take kindly to being cheated out of the proceeds of their endeavours. Inevitably there was a backlash. The biggest early losers, the Feltrim and Gooda Walker Names formed Action Groups to investigate and take legal action against Lloyds. Joe and I were among the Names on these early scandal syndicates and we joined the Action Groups. Later it turned out that our syndicates, bad as they were, suffered no worse than many others which came to light later. Our misfortune turned out in a way to be good fortune, since we were first to get Lloyds into court before the money in the Central Fund ran out. We were therefore given preferential treatment as first past the post candidates when a global settlement between Lloyds and its Names was reached in 1996 – Reconstruction and Renewal – which in effect shared out what was left in the pot and reinsured on-going liabilities for all the pre-1993 years into a new company, Equitas, owned by the Names. This allowed us to resign and withdraw our Lloyds deposits once our post-1992 open years had been closed. Most Names seized the opportunity to get out but Joe and I not only carried on for a few more years but actually increased our underwriting levels, me to £500,000 and then in 1995 to £800,000 and Joe to more than double those levels. Les Brown's construction company had got into difficulties and he had been forced to resign several years earlier. Lucky beggar! The thinking behind my decision to 'write on' was simple. The safest time to fly is just after a big air crash. The cleanest place to eat is in a restaurant that has just reopened after being closed down by the public health inspectors. The best time to buy shares is after a market crash. So, I figured, the syndicates to support were those who had survived and were now operating in a closely monitored market emerging from the trough of a poor insurance cycle.

There was still a real fear that in the face of gung ho activities by opportunist US lawyers Equitas may fail and we may be called on to meet claims from asbestosis litigants in the USA but I made it difficult for them or anyone else to get at the few remaining assets in my name.

For me, the real tragedy of those difficult years was that it had a profound impact on other aspects of my life. Lloyds Names are liable not only for the deposit they lodge. They are liable down to their last pair of cufflinks, as the Chairman quipped during my interview in 1979. He must surely have known then of the cynical "recruit to dilute" plans and that Lloyds were about to hoodwink thousands of new Names to fund the inevitable losses already in the pipeline. Lambs to the slaughter comes to mind. The Chairman's "cufflink" warning came to be viewed as perfunctory. Three hundred years of retained cufflinks acted as a powerful sedative to Names poised to sign up. With the very real threat of personal bankruptcy constantly on my mind my confidence was at a low ebb. I found solace in drink. I couldn't concentrate properly on my business. I turned a blind eye to certain things that were happening and buried my head in the sand because I simply could not at that time face up to any additional stress.

The decision not to resign immediately from Lloyds when we had the opportunity in 1993 did however pay dividends. We did make some modest profits before resigning three years later but we nevertheless came out of our Lloyds adventure hundreds of thousands of pounds worse off!

So how *do* you make a small fortune at Lloyds? Easy – YOU START OFF WITH A BIG ONE!

♣

I didn't forget the prank in the Cumberland Hotel in which Joe Laidler had subjected me to much embarrassment. Some years after the incident we both happened to be in London separately on business and we arranged to meet for a drink in Joe's hotel. I arrived early and sat at a table where I patiently waited until Joe turned up. When he arrived and went over to the bar for a drink he was accosted by a young lady who harassed him unmercifully, making Joe feel decidedly hot under the collar. When he tried to escape she hauled him back and when she picked up one of the drinks he had left on the bar I could see he was becoming angry. I then went over and told Marilyn (for it was her) that enough was enough, rescued Joe from his ordeal and introduced them. Revenge is sweet!

The Lloyds Building in Lime Street WC3, known as the inside out building. All staircases, lifts, service pipes etc were built on the outside to create space inside.

Nine

THE ENEMY WITHIN

Time to start whipping the crack.
Chrissarism

WHATEVER WORKING MOTHERS say to justify themselves you cannot successfully do two jobs. Particularly if those jobs are as important as running a business or raising a family. Something or someone will suffer. Whilst I was busy spinning plates trying to keep on top of work and family needs I was desperate to avoid a staff crisis to compound my domestic crisis so I had paid well and promoted hastily, perhaps too well and too hastily. Some of my panic decisions in these areas were to backfire on me. During my absence from the helm due to my domestic crises in 1977 and 1978 the ship had encountered a few storms and was knocked off course. Once back on the quarter deck I was able to take stock of the situation and it became clear that if further storms were to be ridden, changes had to be made, starting with major surgery at management level.

My style of management had always been collective rather than autonomous. I regarded myself not as a boss but merely a member of a team. I believed that it was important for everyone at every level to feel that they could have an input into the decision making process within their branch and, ultimately therefore, the running and direction of the company. My philosophy was two pronged – firstly, to break down any 'us and them' mentality, and then to create a feeling of belonging and therefore loyalty. I liked to keep my ear to the ground by retaining links with the front line staff and pick up on any Chinese whispers. That way I would get early warning of any signs of discontent and other valuable feedback. No longer able to devote time to working physically at the front line it was important to get feedback from that important customer contact point. I instructed managers to hold regular staff meetings, many of which whenever possible I would attend. Staff would be encouraged to give their frank and honest views on any subject. In order to achieve this, they must be made to feel comfortable in the knowledge that their views would be welcomed and their criticisms not taken personally. It is quite unacceptable for managers, just because they have the title of manager, to pretend they know it all, become aloof and strut their importance as so many do.

I like to think that I set an example, not simply by being approachable – though I think I was – but by being the approacher! By that I mean taking an interest in staff in both their work and as people. How many bosses have announced importantly and pompously "My office door is always open"? How many staff have the courage to respond? No, a good manager leaves his office door open so that he can see and hear what's going on and be ready to get involved in any problems or to assist staff who may be struggling to deal with difficult situations. If appropriate, occasional social contact outside the office would also be helpful provided this wasn't done selectively with only your favourites, making sure always not to get too closely involved. I may have to discipline or dismiss them one day. I found it particularly valuable to find out what the quiet ones were thinking. I remember interviewing for staff at Middlesbrough and selecting a girl who was so shy she didn't say a word during the interview. The others were confident but not at all impressive. After taking a little while to settle in, this particular girl turned up trumps! If you can't improve on silence say nothing! Or, as Abraham Lincoln once said:

Better to remain silent and be thought a fool, than speak and remove all doubt.

Feedback from the 'quiet ones' was, for example, instrumental in us providing uniforms for the staff. The less well-off ones were under pressure from those from wealthier families who were able to afford the latest designer gear. Uniforms were a great leveller in this area and have since become a feature of the non-manual work place. For my Utopian management methods to succeed, I needed to appoint like-minded people! I was to find such animals were a rare species and since cloning was scientifically impossible some of my appointments proved, inevitably I suppose, disappointing. Unable to rely on their ability or in some cases their common sense, I urged managers to adhere to procedures embodied in the set of manuals which had been produced using feedback from the front line and my own years of experience there. These procedure manuals were excellent training aids and were regularly updated following our procedure meetings, the minutes of which were always sent to the managers to discuss with their staff. The idea was to avoid people doing their own thing in their own (inefficient) way. "There is only one best way to do things" was my message.

I had tried my best to direct operations from my enforced ivory tower at home and I introduced an incentive scheme to encourage and retain staff. This was done in consultation with the managers who I assumed would cooperate with its objective, which was to increase turnover which would improve profitability, in which all of us would share. Because of my situation I couldn't afford to lose staff, or so I feared, and had tried to ensure their loyalty with good salaries, company cars and generous expense accounts. Now they had an opportunity to share in the profits and perks in the same way as if they were shareholders like Ian Fletcher. Surely they would identify with my business philosophy and would respond positively.

Our Westgate Road branch was situated in the heartland of Newcastle's motorcycle dealers. Terry Henderson, the manager there, saw this as an opportunity to increase the branch turnover knowing full well that the commission we earned on motor cycle business, sometimes as low as 5%, was well below the margin we needed to break even, let alone make a profit. Nevertheless, seizing the opportunity to make a quick buck, Terry piled on the motorcycle business and under the terms of the bonus scheme we were obliged to pay substantial bonus payments to him, despite the branch being, as a result, unprofitable. Not a dissimilar situation to that in which banks found themselves two decades later when they paid massive bonuses to their executives only to find that their growth too was achieved at the expense of profit. I made a mental note that Terry clearly was not a team player, putting his personal short-term greed before the overall corporate welfare of his branch, and of the company. When I eventually found out what he was up to, I hastily amended the terms of the scheme to exclude business earning less than 10% in commission. What a pity our inept government fails miserably in similarly controlling and regulating our financial institutions. It's not rocket science. Terry was a sharp lad but his card was marked and his days at Arnotts numbered, and he knew it. He left and set up his own brokers business in nearby Silksworth. I admired Terry's enterprise. Many criticise their bosses and have opinions on how the job should be done. Few have the courage to put their actions where their mouths are and set up their own businesses. I liked Terry. He had flair. He demonstrated this one day when a customer came into his office with his dog and Terry went to the counter to attend to him. "Sit!" ordered the customer. The dog obeyed and so did Terry who promptly sat on the floor!

Since our Lloyds syndicates and many of the insurance companies we acted for were based in and around London, I encouraged the development of relationships with them by sending our own underwriting staff to their seminars. I thought it would prove beneficial also for our team to meet their counterparts on their own patches. Robert Newton was given the task of organising a trip to London. They were to catch an early morning train from Edinburgh and Newcastle and I would join them at Darlington. When I got on the train there was no sign of them. In vain I walked the length of the train and back wondering whether I was on the wrong train. I found a seat and decided to make a telephone call when I arrived at Kings Cross. This was of course in pre-mobile phone days. Shortly after taking my seat I looked up to find a sheepish Robert Newton walking towards me. Puzzled, I asked him where everybody was and Robert explained that he had left the arrangements to Alan Crawford and he had booked them into first class. So the boss slummed it while his employees travelled in style, squandering hard earned profit which would affect the bonuses of their colleagues back in the branches working extra hard in their absence. After that I made sure that Alan was last in the pecking order when it came to salary review time.

Dennis Mee, who was appointed manager at Middlesbrough following Dave Smith's promotion to Motor Underwriting Manager, was, like Terry Henderson, an ex-V&G man and they were close friends, fellow conspirators even. Had they been left to their own devices for much longer the power struggle which I suspected was growing under the surface may well have erupted into a confrontation between the ex-V&G men and Ian Fletcher. Dennis also proved to be incapable of playing for the team. Having sat in meetings for hours to decide on a set of standard practices and procedures, Dennis was the type of lad who rarely contributed anything positive. His attitude was insolent. I always felt that he was a little disdainful of what we were trying to achieve, that he would ignore what we had democratically and usually unanimously agreed and then go back to his branch and do his own thing anyway. If he thought he had a better way to operate then he should have given the rest of us the benefit of his wisdom. That's what our meetings were for. This attitude infuriated me. Dennis was the antithesis of my ideal manager. When the time was right, he too would have to go. It wasn't long before an opportunity to expose his arrogance was to present itself during one of my visits to his branch, when my attention was attracted by an irate customer giving one of the girls a hard time. Dennis made no attempt to intervene so I did. The customer had called several times and was now threatening to expose us in the local Evening Gazette because we wouldn't give him a refund of premium on the policy he had cancelled over two months earlier. As he quite rightly pointed out, we wanted his money up front before we would cover him but it was a different story when he wanted money from us. I asked Dennis why this was so and Dennis explained that the insurance company concerned were very inefficient and had not yet sent a credit note to us. Not good enough. This was not unique. The issue had been brought up at our meetings and a solution found. Instead of having an unhappy customer on our hands and instead of him wasting our time constantly calling in the office or telephoning, a decision had been made and agreed unanimously that we would calculate the refund ourselves and issue a cheque there and then. I called for the branch chequebook and gave the customer his refund with profuse apologies and an assurance that such a situation would not arise in future. But with Dennis breaking the rules how could I be sure it wouldn't? He would have to go sooner rather than later. He was guilty of a blatant disregard for agreed and well documented company procedure but not only that, of the even more culpable offence of ignoring the plight of the young counter clerk who was having to take abuse from a customer after I had stressed repeatedly that young inexperienced staff were not paid enough to put up with such treatment. The managers were. I didn't expect them to be cowardly and hide behind young skirts.

Anarchy was not confined to branch level. Ian and Iain, Fletcher and Ferguson, did not like each other. I suppose in those days it was too much to expect otherwise between a devout Catholic and a true blue Glasgow Rangers fanatic. Had I been available to mediate I'm sure I would have got the best out of them but leaving them alone and unsupervised as the only two active directors in the company during my enforced absence was a recipe for trouble. Things came to a head when Ian Fletcher sneaked a look into Iain Ferguson's briefcase and discovered a complicated case file which had been allowed to get into an almost irretrievable position, leaving us exposed to a professional negligence claim. I was proud of the fact that our professional indemnity insurers had never been called upon and was naturally dismayed when I was informed by Ian Fletcher of his fellow director's incompetence. Had I been around I have no doubt that Iain would have consulted me over the case in question and it would have been sorted out. I suppose Iain was too proud to admit to Ian Fletcher that he couldn't handle it, though I doubt whether Ian could have done so either. Ian Fletcher's triumphant discovery led eventually to Iain Ferguson's resignation. I was sorry to lose him because he was well liked and respected by the staff and by the insurance companies we dealt with. We lost in the process also two friends – Iain and Pat his wife. Business decisions can at times be brutal.

With so much disruption and disorder at higher levels it is surprising how the Arnott company survived during this period. Even more surprising perhaps was how it continued to progress. Or perhaps not. My emphasis on sound recruiting and staff training was paying off. We might have been weak on Chiefs – but we were strong on Indians.

It wasn't only the staff who had benefited from our training programme. One particular training video had a big influence on me too and helped me to find a way forward in my management crisis. The video in question featured the ex MD of the Avis Corporation of the USA whose name I can't recall. Let's just call him MD. One of MD's thought provoking philosophies, which I took to heart, dealt with attitude. He reckoned that when someone starts a new job they should work with the mentality that they were actually the owners of the company. If that company was worth working for then such an attitude would be quickly recognised and rewarded. If on the other hand this was not the case, then give it three years maximum and then move on to a different company. How profound this philosophy is. So perceptive and so true in my situation at that time. The difference was that I had dished out the promotions and the rewards to some people before finding out whether they shared this philosophy. In his video, MD also revealed to me the way to replace my unwanted managers. He had been called on by Avis shareholders to rescue the company, which was on the verge of collapse. He listened patiently as the board of directors trotted out their excuses and their reasons for the company's plight and to their surprise, given the urgency of the situation, MD called the next board meeting for two months hence. This next meeting lasted no more than five minutes. MD announced that he had found out what was wrong with the company. "You and you and you," he said, pointing to each director. "You are as of now relieved of your office. Leave your company credit cards and car keys at reception. I have arranged taxis to take you home." The shocked and angry directors warned MD that he couldn't run the company without them. MD told them that was now his problem, not theirs. During the period between his first and the directors' last board meeting MD had spent his time with the staff who worked at various levels within the company – the mechanics who repaired and serviced the cars, the drivers who delivered them, the people in the depots who cleaned them and the sales staff who dealt with the customers. He selected a cross section of these front line employees and established a fresh board of directors who knew what they were talking about. The rest is history. Avis is now established as a massive global corporation.

How I would have enjoyed working with someone like MD whose philosophies I share. Be patient. Don't act hastily even if provoked. Bide your time. People in a false sense of security, given enough rope, will usually hang themselves. Be prepared to act when it suits you not others and only when it causes minimum disruption. Most of all as it says in the hymn – 'Do not strive.' Nothing's ever worth a heart attack. I soon discovered that we too at Arnotts had more than our fair share of unsung heroes and heroines who were to prove more than adequate replacements for the old school. But the cull wasn't over yet.

For twenty years Ian Fletcher had been a reliable colleague. That's why I had given him a 10% shareholding in Marshall Arnott Ltd, and later a third ownership in Wheatsheaf Coachworks, the car repair workshop I set up with John Baker. I also gave him 25% of Northern Admin Services Ltd (NASLIM) our new uninsured loss and claims recovery service which had real potential as society became more litigation conscious. A single lad with few interests outside of work Ian was truly a workaholic and never took normal holidays. In one respect I was lucky to have someone so dedicated but his single minded introverted overzealous behaviour was abnormal and unnatural. This made me feel uneasy at times. Was he capable of making balanced judgements? Staff would often arrive at work to find the office completely reorganised by Ian who had spent half the night moving their desks around and relocating filing cabinets and other furniture. No discussion or consultation was involved and usually no improvement achieved – often the opposite. The general feeling was that he did it to fill his time in. I didn't interfere. I didn't have time to and I was reluctant to knock his enthusiasm. Organisation is important of course but not at the expense of the productive side of the business which entailed keeping the customers happy and negotiating competitive terms with insurance companies and Lloyds. Ian rarely got involved in those more important areas. A serious minded individual he didn't mix well and was not at ease outside his cosy zone as a back room boy.   He considered himself to be quite a righteous and upstanding person and could at times be quite pompous. He lacked, what they call in Spain "simpatico" with people. An example of this was to manifest itself during one of our visits to Glasgow accompanied by Brian who was to do some sales training, although it wasn't strictly necessary since the girls there seemed to be doing pretty well without it. I suppose, speaking perfectly as my wife would say, the visit was largely a staff relations exercise, an excuse to have a long business lunch in the nice restaurant next door to the office and after work to take the girls for a few (?) drinks in the nearby Press Bar next door to the Glasgow Herald headquarters. Run by three brothers, Gerry, Alex and Des and frequented by a host of "characters" this old fashioned Glasgow drinking den was the scene of many a good evening on our visits there. The girls and I could sense a bit of a strained atmosphere between Ian and Brian.   This, we learned, was due to an earlier situation when Ian had taken Brian to one side and piously given him a stern talking to for using the "F" word in front of the girls. This is Glasgow we are talking about remember! When the girls heard about this in the Press Bar later they turned round and told Ian not to be so fucking pompous. Though he shouldn't have been, Ian was shocked. He bristled but said nothing. Because I was present the girls felt relaxed enough to say what they felt. Besides it was outside office hours. Good for them.   There was no place for pomposity in my Company.

The advent of computers in the nineteen seventies and eighties was manna from heaven for Ian. Here was something new and exciting he could really get his teeth into. Whilst recognising some of the obvious benefits of computerisation, I treated with some suspicion Ian's enthusiastic conviction that it was the answer to all our problems. Storage and quick retrieval of client data would certainly improve customer service and ultimately save us money by cutting back on space and manpower. However, such a huge step needed to be undertaken with caution and introduced gradually in parallel with our tried and tested paper system, in which important documents were stored. I preferred to postpone the decision until I was in a position to become involved but under pressure from Ian, whose attitude was persuasively positive I gave the green light for the installation of an experimental pilot system at Sunderland. The system chosen was Cheshire Data Systems, mainly because they were working on a programme which would produce straightforward car insurance quotations even though at that stage this would be of little use to us since we had negotiated non-standard preferential premiums with most of our insurers and early computer quote systems compared only standard premium rates. Let loose with his new toy, Ian submerged himself in this new technology and became increasingly excited about its value and potential, closing his eyes I suspect to any possible negative aspects. Working night and day familiarising himself with the system, he was impatient to see it up and running. Unfortunately, true to form he didn't, in his haste to 'go live', familiarise the staff or give them proper re-training. Nor did he consider too seriously any possible downsides, such was his blinkered determination to demonstrate what a wonderful Utopia his baby would create, almost overnight.

Now the whole ethos of my Company had been built on personal service. The customers paid the wages. They were the most important people in our business. Customer loyalty is vital to growth. No point in having good new business figures if the existing customers were not renewing their policies. The computer didn't seem to understand that. Not in the hasty and autonomous way Ian had set it up. To say that Ian was obsessed would not be understating the case. He spent most of his life sat in front of a screen. In order to bulldoze his baby into use he discarded our tried and tested paper system to force the shell-shocked staff to use the computer. Inevitably there were problems and I was alerted to them when a long-standing customer insisted on speaking to me personally. He was telephoning from Corby in Northamptonshire where hundreds of local miners had moved following the pit closures in the North East. He had been with Arnotts for twenty years and enjoyed hearing a friendly Wearside voice whenever he needed advice on his insurances. "Why don't you want my business anymore?" he asked me. "I don't want to leave Arnotts." I reassured him that of course we wanted his business and how important it was to us. I was horrified and furious when he explained what had happened. Because of limitations in the computer system we were, apparently, no longer able to correspond with clients as we had in the past. Ian had devised his infamous "Call and Discuss" letter which was sent to clients every time there was a query on their cases. Having received this letter the Corby customer had telephoned to find out what the problem was and to explain that since he now lived two hundred miles away, he couldn't call into the office. He had been advised by Ian that he should therefore insure his car locally. A clear case of customer versus computer. We didn't want customers who didn't fit the system. No question of making the computer fit the customer. Heaven knows how many customers we had lost in this way.

Alarm bells were ringing. I asked the staff for their views, which confirmed my worst fears. They had been indoctrinated into thinking that the computer was more important than the client and that the problem wasn't confined to customers living outside the area. Many local ones had expressed annoyance after receiving this letter, which had led them to believe there may be a major problem. Some had taken time off work to call into the office only to find that the query was trivial and could have been dealt with by post or telephone or by asking the wife to call into the office when she was in town. There are BPO's (Business Prevention Officers) in many organisations. We clearly had one in ours.

I had to put other plans on hold and spend time I could ill afford in sorting out the chaos Ian had caused. With such a cavalier attitude towards the customers I could no longer leave him to his own devices. He seemed to have no concept of how much effort by so many people went into winning new customers. He was living in a different world to the rest of us. I could not continue to allow him to undo so much of the good work done by the rest of the staff. He was dangerous. I put a stop to his involvement in the branch and suggested he concentrated on NASLIM and Wheatsheaf Coachworks where I hoped he couldn't do any serious damage. I was wrong.

Fortunately by then some of the other members of staff had become familiar with the computer and together we were able to make some changes, albeit within the limitations of the system, and come up with a much more customer friendly approach. All it took was a bit of common sense, consultation and an awareness of the customers' needs. I devised a multi question form – the staff called it an 'F' form for some reason. This contained a numbered list of all the more common queries to which we required answers and was enclosed with a computer produced letter indicating which particular query required the customer's attention. The Call & Discuss letter was scrapped.

I was astounded at the extent of damage Ian had caused at Sunderland and was puzzled how and why he had done so. His behaviour was incomprehensible. There were several strange things happening during this period. I couldn't quite put my finger on it but there was certainly something wrong. It never crossed my mind that Ian could be deliberately creating difficulties. He did some irrational things like having some different car stickers printed for no logical reason. It was as if he wanted to undermine everything I did. As if he resented my involvement in my own Company. He seemed envious that the staff held me in respect rather than him. Was he disappointed when I returned to work? Had he during my absence enjoyed the power? Was he hoping to become the main man? I don't know what was going through his mind. There were many disturbing things about his behaviour.

The arrangement I had with Wheatsheaf Coachworks (WC) was that Arnotts would send claimants there who needed repairs to their cars and in the case of non-fault accidents a courtesy hire car would be supplied on credit. It was understood and agreed that if the third party claim was for some reason unsuccessful WC would waive their hire charge. Customers would in effect get a free hire car. Ignoring our gentlemen's agreement, letters threatening legal proceedings were sent from WC to Arnott customers provoking angry responses from them claiming that they had not been told by WC that they may be expected to pay for their 'courtesy' car. Another example of Ian Fletcher trying to cause mischief? I was later told that he had acquired some cars of his own which were being hired out in preference to the WC cars in which I had a beneficial interest. I never found out whether our partner John Baker was a party to this. Having discovered these acts of treachery my involvement in WC was no longer sustainable. I couldn't work in partnership with people capable of such deceit and dishonesty. They could no longer be trusted. The WC business was my idea. I saw the opportunity. I was a friend of John Baker who had the practical expertise and I introduced him to Ian. I generously gave them a third share each, believing that I could leave them to run the business and we could all eventually share in its success. Without the money which I and Arnotts introduced we could not have bought the property and the equipment. Without the Arnott customers it could not have got itself established. All this was forgotten. My generosity was kicked in my face. In disgust I withdrew from the partnership and withdrew the money I had put in to make it viable – and the accrued profits which I had left in the partnership to help its cash flow. They asked if they could repay it in instalments. In view of the shameful way they had treated me I should have refused and caused them problems like they had caused me. But I didn't. I should have had an angry confrontation with John and Ian but what good would that do? The damage was done and I just wanted to get on with my life. In the back of my mind was the thought that perhaps Ian Fletcher may do the honourable thing too and gracefully surrender his Arnott shares. He didn't. Had WC been a limited company, having resigned as a director I could have held on to my shares as a bargaining tool to recover Ian's Arnott shares. Failing that, the shares would have made me a tidy profit when twelve years later a retail park was built on the WC site and the property was sold for a substantial sum.

After all I had done for Ian, his behaviour had sickened me and I just wanted him out of my life. He had caused me enough heartache at a particularly stressful time. I consoled myself with the thought that with the money I withdrew from WC I could increase my underwriting at Lloyds. Talk about a double bloody whammy!

I still had the problem also with Ian's involvement at NASLIM which had been relocated to Albany House in Washington, Co Durham, and he was still a director and shareholder of Marshall Arnott Ltd. It wasn't going to be easy to get rid of him. But help was on the way.

WE HAVE READ YOUR PROPOSAL...

...AND ARE GIVING IT

SERIOUS CONSIDERATION.

(IAN FLETCHER, TERRY HENDERSON & DENNIS MEE

JUST AFTER I HAD CLOSED A MEETING AND LEFT)

Ten

ARNOTT pcl

*You can't expect to succeed beyond your wildest dreams
until you dare to dream something wild.*
Scott Sorrell

MOST GROWING BUSINESSES reach a critical point when, if you don't get the blend and the balance right, they become vulnerable. Two examples of this were Les Brown, my fellow "Name" at Lloyds and Jack Stewart, Brian's Glasgow pal. Their respective construction companies failed, yet both were brilliant builders. Les spent too much time on the books and not enough on the bricks. Jack spent too much time on the bricks and not enough on the books.

Looking back and trying to analyse my company's situation in the nineteen-eighties, if I had to give myself marks for market awareness, marketing, motivation and man management, they would be marvellous. Minimal for modesty then! For money management however, they would be moderate – mediocre even. In this life I have found out that jobs you are good at, you enjoy and can quickly accomplish with ease and efficiency. On the other hand, we struggle with things we don't enjoy and in these areas our tasks take up a disproportionate amount of our time. My company was generating a lot of money but I was not using this to best advantage. I played the money markets to a certain extent but in the area of finance generally, I was inefficient. I found myself after the management shake-up with, effectively, a board of directors of one – Me. Ian Fletcher had been moved sideways into the uninsured loss claims operation as a damage limitation exercise until I had time to deal with him and, like the Avis MD, I had promoted some of my unsung heroes. Robert Newton became General Manager, Les Wood and Ken Lee, Regional Managers of Teesside and Tyne & Wear respectively and of course Marilyn Thomson was more than holding the fort in Scotland. Dave Smith was in charge of motor quotations in England.

Despite having in our midst and working against everything I was trying to achieve, a fifth columnist (a war time expression for an enemy sympathiser or a spy) the company was nevertheless growing. In particular, our office in Borough Road, Middlesbrough was running out of space and would have a limited life span. Anticipating the inevitable need for larger premises I had seized the opportunity to buy three derelict properties, 212, 214 and 216 Linthorpe Road, Middlesbrough's major thoroughfare. The plan was to sit on these properties, which had been acquired very cheaply, until I or the company could afford to develop them. I didn't realise that the Local Authority was invested with the power to enforce development, which is probably why they were so cheap, and after a few months a dilapidation order was served on me. This required the owner, by law, to at least carry out the repairs and renovations necessary to make the properties look presentable. They were, I admit, a bit of an eyesore. However, this wasn't what I had in mind. A full-scale development would be costly and I wasn't quite ready to embark on a property venture which would demand a substantial call on my time and probably a bank loan. I had already pledged a lot of money to Lloyds. There was of course a substantial pot of money in the company account made up mainly of premiums paid to us in advance which were not due to be paid to insurance companies until they had issued their policies, which for some, would be up to three months since the first cover note was issued. In effect we were enjoying up to three months credit, which meant that, allowing for some of this being passed on to customers, about twenty per cent of our turnover was earning interest for us in addition to our commissions. This money however was held in trust and I couldn't risk raiding this pot for such a speculative venture as property development of which I had no experience.

I called in a small builder friend of my father's to tidy up the frontages of the properties in the hope that this would satisfy the Council. It didn't. A substantial reconstruction was necessary which involved structural steelwork. A specialist, Max Cook, was called in. Max was very helpful but warned me that my one man band jobbing builder would not be up to the job. I asked for his advice and he recommended Edwin Davis Cleveland Ltd, a small local construction company. A meeting on site was arranged with their director Brooks Mileson and plans were drawn up by Mike Graham of Blue Point Design for the type of development I had envisaged, which would maximise the value of the property. Arnotts would occupy the first floor accessed through an imposing street level entry door, and the more easily rentable ground floor units would be retail outlets thus ensuring maximum occupancy. The cost would be kept to a minimum by doing the job on a cost plus basis, where a pre-agreed profit was set and everything else was charged at cost. I was to attend all the site meetings to be in on the decision making process regarding type and quality of materials used and other issues affecting the cost. In addition to Brooks, Mike Graham and Max Cook and foreman Robbie Henderson, I was to make the acquaintance of decorator Ronnie Evans who was later to become a friend and fellow golfer. The financial situation was explained to Brooks, who persuaded me that the risk factor would be minimal. With this reassurance I dipped into the company kitty. Sure enough as it turned out, the asset value of the property exceeded the capital outlay. I was impressed with Brooks' financial knowledge. He was, he claimed, a qualified company accountant. We had, he said, a mutual friend in Toby White although I hadn't seen Toby or his wife Marlene for some years because Chris didn't like them and with good reason. Marlene had rudely embarrassed her at a Masonic dinner and Toby had, she told me, once tried to proposition her, a fact she kept from me and which would undoubtedly have influenced a decision I was to make later.

Brooks displayed a keen interest in my company, which was by then quite substantial and a household name thanks to our WE

ARNOTT INSURED car stickers. He volunteered his assistance in the financial side of Arnotts and I was only too ready to have some help in this area, which was not my forte and which had been hitherto Jack Reed's responsibility. Brooks undoubtedly had a talent in the area of commercial finance, a talent that my company was crying out for, since I found myself more and more bogged down in this time consuming and unproductive area. Brooks clearly recognised an opportunity for himself and his company to benefit from an association with the region's leading personal insurance provider. Obviously keen to ingratiate himself with the Arnott organisation he did everything he could to impress me, including giving my eldest son a lucrative Saturday job in his builders yard, which James thoroughly enjoyed.

I came to rely on Brooks' gratuitous help more and more and we talked about the possibility of him becoming our Financial Director, a post he was only too eager to accept. Before authorising the appointment however, I would give him a challenge. Get rid of Ian Fletcher and Brooks could replace him as a director. I don't know how he did it but he did. Despite his blatant misconduct his dismissal came as a shock to Ian who must have thought that having taken no immediate action, I would allow the matter to be overlooked. After Brooks had spoken to him Ian wrote to me twice. In his letters he more than confirmed my suspicions. For a long time he admitted, he had been doing things and saying things to deliberately cause me embarrassment and problems – as if I didn't have enough already. He had been to St Benets and confessed everything and he asked me to forgive him too. I have forgiven him. But perhaps the church's and Ian's idea of forgiveness differs from mine. I think I was expected to say, "Oh, that's all right then. I forgive you. Have your job back and we'll carry on as if nothing had happened." No, I couldn't do that. Ian had demonstrated that he was capable of irrational behaviour. I couldn't take the risk of continuing to run the company whilst constantly looking over my shoulder to see if there was a knife sticking in my back. To quote the old Jewish proverb, *"Rejoice not at your enemy's fall. But do not rush to pick him up either."* To Ian's credit he did come clean and owned up to his failings. It can't have been easy. But this kind of behaviour is beyond my comprehension. I can understand people being devious for selfish reasons. To use me and my company to achieve their own personal gain and ambitions as was about to happen. What is incomprehensible is that someone should want to damage me and my Company just for the sake of it. What motivates people to do this sort of thing without any rational justification? Is it resentment? Is it jealousy? I was to ask the same questions eleven years later.

When Brooks joined the company it was in a healthy state and its growth was self-perpetuating. I needed to ease the pressure on the Middlesbrough Branch which covered the whole of Teesside and which included in its client base enough Redcar and Stockton motorists to justify opening branches in these nearby towns. This gave me an opportunity to appoint two new managers, Kath Callaghan and Debi Craggs which sent a message to our young ambitious workforce that if they did well then there was a career path for them within the Arnott organisation. I was content to see the company evolve in this way. Brooks on the other hand wanted to accelerate the growth, excited by the prospect of increasing the bank balance beyond the two million pounds which he had achieved by settling our accounts in a more efficient way and also excited no doubt, by the prospect of his own company Edwin Davis Limited gaining the contracts for fitting out the new branches. Our ambitious management team were also obviously keen to see the company grow. I was cautious. I had already experienced a situation where due to personal circumstances beyond my control I had almost lost control. I feared a repetition. And after thirty-four years in the insurance business I wasn't sure that this was what I really wanted.

Brooks Mileson may have been many things but he was no fool and he could be very persuasive. He touched the right spot when he said to me that there was no reason why Arnotts could not in a few years' time be floated on the Stock Market. I had, many years ago in my private dreams, thought vaguely of the possibility of an Arnott plc which would mean a big pay day and perhaps more importantly the handing over of corporate responsibility to the City and a vindication of all the effort, hard work and of the time I felt I had stolen from my family. Yes, the thought excited me. The prospect of the commitment and responsibility of achieving it didn't. Besides, I had just won my first golf medal and I wanted more time for enjoyment, not less. I knew I was at a crossroads. The decision wasn't going to be easy. Selling out meant deserting the staff whose futures I had assured them were in good hands – mine. They trusted me. Could I abandon them to the vagaries of new owners? But unlike on other occasions when I had considered getting out, this was a good time to sell. Swintons, one of our competitors and a national chain broker who, like us, had started up in a small office, theirs in Swinton, Lancashire, had recently been taken over by the massive Sun Alliance Insurance Group who were looking for further acquisitions. On the few subsequent occasions I met their then very wealthy proprietor he didn't have a care in the world. The temptation for me to get out too, was strong. I didn't of course share my thoughts with the staff or with Brooks and eventually I decided I couldn't do it. I couldn't pack in now. I would go for it, but not without grave misgivings. Could the new young management team handle the pressure? Could I trust Brooks?

Oh, and by the way, there isn't an error in the title of this Chapter. You will find out later what pcl stands for.

Eleven

MORTON HOUSE

It stands out like a bare thumb.
Chrissarism

FOLLOWING THE DISAPPOINTING response by some members of staff to my workers' co-operative style of management I realised I could no longer expect them to have the level of commitment I had hoped for and had tried to encourage. My attitude and approach to business had always been that the Company was more important than the individual and I suppose it was naïve of me to expect others to feel the same. I put up with situations I wouldn't expect my staff to. This attitude was particularly evident when it came to an office. Mine would be anywhere there was room. When a new branch opened I could work from there until it grew and needed the space. Then I would move on. I was like an executive nomad. For some reason the subject cropped up when I was playing golf at Chester-le-Street with Brian, Peter Peyton and our regular four ball partner Tim Nicholson who lived in Groom Cottage in Fencehouses, near Durham which had, centuries earlier, been the house of the groomsman to the Lords of the Manor who had earlier occupied nearby Morton House. I mentioned my nomadic corporate existence to Tim and how one day I would like to find somewhere to locate our group executive offices, preferably out in the country with easy parking. "Why don't you have a word with Frances Berriman?" suggested Tim. "She might be persuaded to sell." Tim explained that Mrs Berriman lived alone in that big old house and was under pressure from her son Geoffrey, concerned for the welfare and vulnerability of his then elderly mother, to find somewhere smaller and less remote. Tim later introduced me to Mrs Berriman. I explained to her the purpose of my interest in the house and that I didn't intend to convert it into flats or a nursing home which she feared would become its fate once she moved out. She was persuaded to have a further meeting with Brooks and I, at which we assured her that we would preserve Morton House's status as a dwelling for which it had a long and distinguished heritage.

Built in circa 1340 by Petrus de Morton, the house stood in its own ten acres of private woodland and lawned gardens with separate walled produce garden and orchard and accessed by a narrow bumpy axle unfriendly track from Fencehouses Front Street. The original owner was I believe one of the Prince Bishops in those medieval days when County Durham's entire population was no more than 51,000, half of which was later wiped out by the Black Death. The House boasts a series of prestigious subsequent owners, including the Lumleys from 1406-37, Richard Errington c 1490 and the family of Sir William Balasyse Kt from 1525-1678. It was rebuilt by the Smith family of

West Herrington in 1709 in the reign of Queen Anne and the Smith family crest bearing this date still exists above the front door. It was then sold to Major General John George Lambton whose family occupied it for many years. In the late nineteenth century a fire damaged the top of the house and the third storey was removed. The name shown on the deeds from 1920 is A Kirkup, a nominee owner on behalf of a local colliery company and, after nationalisation, became the property of the National Coal Board until 1961 when it was bought by Mr Berriman, a local builder.

Little wonder that Mrs Berriman was reluctant to sell this beautiful house in which she had clearly been so happy for so many years, surrounded by her extensive collection of lovely antique furnishings and artefacts acquired by her husband during his extensive travels abroad. However, she did eventually agree to sell it to us, persuaded finally perhaps by our promise to allow it to continue to be used for charity fund raising, mainly on behalf of the Children's Society for which she was a Patron. After we acquired the house she was our honoured guest there on a number of subsequent occasions, including an Antiques Road Show held one evening on behalf of her charity at which an expert from Sotheby's politely gave his opinion on the load of old junk we brought along with high hopes and unrealistic expectations. An old oil painting treasured by my grandfather received a thumbs down because it didn't bear the artist's name which had disappeared when someone in the family had callously butchered the canvas when removing it to use the frame for another picture. The evening, notwithstanding, was good fun and most enjoyably different.

We bought the house in the name of the Albany Uninsured Loss Recovery Company which had replaced NASLIM. Ideal in every respect for our new HQ it was, I believed, a very good investment because of its potential in other respects. If we were ever to move on then it would also make an ideal venue for functions. In fact I was soon to have an opportunity to use it for that very purpose. Daughter Liz chose to get married in Las Vegas on 11th August 1992, the day before my father died. We didn't tell her of course until she returned from her honeymoon. A month later, on the 11th September, we organised for her and her new husband a splendid wedding bash at Morton House. Pat Tiffany, one of our senior staff members, laid on a beautiful display of flowers and a five star buffet and I organised some party games and various activities designed to give the newlyweds and their guests a memorable occasion. We succeeded in doing so beyond our own expectations, which served to reinforce my conviction that Morton House could have a post Albany/Arnotts role as a venue for weddings and other social functions.

The house was to provide the perfect setting for a number of other events which we organised and I must pay tribute to the staff there for their help and to Robert Newton for his boundless energy and contribution and again to Pat Tiffany and her helpers. Pat made a better hostess than a clerkess and had surely missed her vocation. Fancy dress Christmas parties for the senior staff and their partners were great fun with Chris and I dressed as Father and Mother Christmas. It's a Knockout contests on the lawn were also immensely popular with the managers and senior staff and did much to cement staff loyalty, team spirit and maintain morale. I organised annual Arnott Masters golf days at the nearby Chester le Street Golf Club for the brown Masters Jacket and après golf dinners in the ballroom back at Morton House with Kevin Connolly, the talented impersonator and star of BBC's 'Dead Ringers' TV show as after dinner speaker. I knew Kevin from Acklam Park Cricket & Rugby Club in MIddlesbrough and gave him what I believe was his first professional engagement a few years earlier when I invited him to perform at the Norton TA Centre where I sponsored a local junior amateur boxing tournament. Kevin who can't stand the sight of blood waited outside until it was his turn to perform during the half time interval, which unfortunately coincided with the mad scramble for the free supper. The tournament was a success. Alas, the entertainment wasn't. Kevin, I'm afraid, couldn't compete with the pie and peas and the general hubbub from the balcony where they were being served and he found himself isolated in the boxing ring. His act was far too sophisticated for the occasion and someone threw a pie crust into the ring. This was the signal for others to use Kevin for target practice. I later apologised to him for my organisational error. He told me that he wouldn't have minded so much if they'd been Upex pies! (Upex was the name of a famous and particularly delicious Teesside meat pie.)

At the first Arnott Masters dinner I found Kevin's performance, or at least part of it, again disappointing. I just couldn't see what was so funny about one particular take off, yet the rest of the guests were in stitches. It wasn't until afterwards, when I asked him what it was all about, that I discovered he had been impersonating *me*!

Among the many excellent social occasions hosted at Morton House were the thirtieth and thirty fifth anniversary parties for Arnott Insurance. The latter featured "entertainment" by the Shakin' Vicars, a heavy metal band in which Brooks' eldest son Paul played lead guitar. But with the possible exception of Liz's wedding (for personal reasons) by far the most extravagant and memorable event was my Geordie Nite, described by one of the guests as the mother of all parties. In fact there were two Geordie Nites. The first was for family and friends and acted as a dress rehearsal for the big corporate night a week later and also served as a reciprocal thank you for all the various parties and functions I had been invited to over the years by our guests that evening. The second, on the 12th September 1990 was a celebration of thirty years of Arnott Insurance to which all our business associates were invited, including many Lloyds Underwriters and their insurance company equivalents, in appreciation of all the cooperation they had given us in maintaining our competitive edge in the market. Guests were greeted by a Geordie piper, enjoyed a gourmet Geordie buffet which included traditional Stottie Cake, Black and Pease Puddings and little fishies on dishies. Our guests enjoyed a host of activities including target golf, clay pigeon shooting and croquet in the grounds and inside, a Geordie quiz, a yard of ale contest and entertainment by a Geordie folk singer and by local comedian Little Billy Fane. The volume and content of cards and letters we received afterwards were testimony to the resounding success of these occasions.

Morton House was indeed a marvellous venue for social functions but it served also as an ideal location for staff training sessions, senior staff meetings, headquarters for Gerrard O'Connor's Arnott Commercial Ltd and had many other practical functions. We were privileged to be able to occupy, albeit for a relatively short period of time, such a beautiful house with such an interesting history, my research into which afforded a fascinating glimpse into the past. Allow me to quote a brief extract from the lengthy and ponderous will of Richarde Belassis made in 1596 in which he painstakingly accounted for and bequeathed every single item of the house contents:

To my other two neces, cc marks apiece towards ther marriges, and if they, or eyther of them, shall be bestowed in marrige, before my deathe, that then I geve unto that partie so bestowed, only 30/- as ther other sisters have. To my said two neces, all the beddes, in the owld heighe chamber, at Morton, over the owld parler ther, with all hangings on the walles, in that chamber, the great presser ther, and the two chests, with the linings in them, and also to eyther of them one little playne whit silver bowle, to drink in, and VII plaine silver spones apiece.

I don't know whether Mr Bellasis was just an old fusspot or whether it was then the norm to identify each and every possession in wills. I found it fascinating and I suppose in five hundred years' time our language will appear quaint too.

The name of the Belasis family who occupied the house in the sixteenth and seventeenth Centuries derives from the historic Manor of Belasis near Billingham on Teesside. Their family crest can be seen in the church of St Andrews Auckland at South Church Co. Durham. The most famous member of the family was Miss Mary Balasis of Brancepeth Castle near Durham who lived in the eighteenth Century and fell in love with Bobby Shaftoe a County Durham MP, from which story the Geordie folksong originates. She is said to have sung the words *"He'll come back to marry me"* but when he did come back from sea he married someone else and Mary is said to have died from a broken heart.

Within Morton House I also finally secured for myself a splendid and permanent office in what was hitherto Mrs Berriman's bedroom, with lovely views over the lawn and woods – and the pheasants, but that's another story.[1]

**The Hostesses. Kathryn Stones, Jane Grant and Julie Barnett.
Geordie Nite, 12th September 1990**

---

[1] Related in Volume I – *Social Domestic & Pleasure.*

Twelve

ARNOTT CUSTOMERS IMPORTANT

Everybody knew how to do it
Anybody could have done it
They all thought **Somebody** would do it
So **Nobody** did it
D.A.

A S EVERYBODY KNOWS, the boss has nothing to do. Except that is, to decide what is to be done. To tell someone to do it. To check up to see if it has been done. To listen to excuses from the person who should have done it. To follow up a second time to find that it has been done incorrectly. To point out how it should have been done. To conclude that since it is now done it might as well be left as it is. To worry about having to carry the can for someone else's mistake. To wonder if it is not time to get rid of the person who cannot do a thing correctly. To ponder whether it is worth going through all the red tape and possibly an industrial tribunal. To remember that the person at fault has a wife, seven children and a mortgage. To reflect that no other executive in the world would put up with him and that in all probability his successor would be just as bad, or worse. To consider how much simpler and better it would have been done had he done it himself and to wish he worked for somebody else.

Before giving Brooks a directorship in Arnotts I had already rewarded him for his help in a number of ways. He was given a share in the Albany ULR company which had replaced NASLIM when this operation was, pre Morton House, moved to Albany House in

Washington, Co Durham, and I had given his building company Edwin Davis Ltd the contract for the construction of my workshop units. The Finance Act of 1980 had introduced very attractive tax incentives for individuals who were prepared to invest in small industrial units to encourage small business start-ups. I knew of an ideal site for such a development, right next door to Wheatsheaf Coachworks in Monk Street, Sunderland, which I was able to acquire on long lease from Sunderland Council. Four units were constructed and rented out which, in addition to the tax relief on my capital outlay, provided me with a rental income too. Mike Graham had put the idea forward, designed the units and managed them for me, in return for which I gave him a third share in a new company Arngrove Development Co Ltd, Brooks being the other shareholder. In addition to managing my personal and corporate properties Arngrove was set up to take advantage of the expansion plans envisaged for Arnotts. The Linthorpe Road, Middlesbrough development was to be a model for future branches. My idea was to acquire similar High Street properties in other towns and cities where new branches were to be opened. Ground floor lettings are never a problem but, by always ensuring secondary first floor occupancy by Arnotts the asset value of the properties would be enhanced since the value of commercial property is determined largely by the rental income it produces. It couldn't fail. Could it? Fortunately some of the properties were bought in the name of my pension fund from which I was to benefit many years later.

The Albany ULR company had as its shareholders myself, Brooks and John McArdle, the solicitor who handled the bulk of our lucrative ULR claims, particularly those which involved personal injury. To be accurate my shares were in Chris's name in order to ring fence them from what was becoming an increasingly predatory Lloyds. John also put his share in his wife's name. I don't know his reason for this but it was a decision he was later to bitterly regret.

At this point Marshall Arnott Ltd was in a healthy position with branches in Sunderland, Glasgow, Newcastle, Middlesbrough, Stockton-on-Tees and Redcar. With our reputation within the insurance industry at its height, with potential managers within the workforce and with our bank balance at an all-time high, there existed an ideal platform from which expansion could evolve. We had a property portfolio, two more ancillary companies to feed off the Arnott client base and Chris's brother Phillip was also making a living with his car hire company based in South Shields and serving the Tyne and Wear clients. The Teesside area was served by Ring Road Motor Company in Darlington, the proprietor of which, Malcolm Burgess, was a friend of John McArdle.

I envisaged an evolutionary expansion. I feared a repetition of the situation which I had experienced previously in which I had almost lost control of my Company and my enthusiasm for the planned expansion was tempered with caution. But it was Brooks' turn to be the man in a hurry and he and our management team with the exuberance of youth, were keen to be part of a robust expansion programme. The prospect of a regular supply of shop fitting contracts for Edwin Davis Ltd was also no doubt part of Brooks' motivation. In considering the proposed expansion two things in particular came to mind. In view of Ian Fletcher's behaviour I did not think it was fair that he should reap the benefits of any future growth of new branches within the Marshall Arnott Company of which he held a ten per cent share. I also thought that since Brooks was to take on much of the responsibility for such growth then he should be tied in with a share of the fruits of his labour. I therefore proposed that all new offices in the future would be opened not as branches of Marshall Arnott Ltd but in the name of two new companies, Arnott Insurance Services in Scotland and Arnott Insurance Services (North East) Ltd in England in which Brooks would be given shareholdings. With the Jack Reed situation in mind I insisted that any new ventures in the future would be set up not with equal shareholdings but with me as the major shareholder in any English companies and Brooks as major shareholder in any Scottish companies. A hopeless optimist, I had learned nothing from my Jack Reed and Ian Fletcher experiences.

Having disposed of Ian Fletcher, Brooks' power lust was revealed to me when he urged me to also squeeze out Robert Newton. I made it quite clear that this was out of the question. I wanted Arnotts to be run by insurance men not by accountants or people with no up-front experience. So when the first new branch of the new era was opened in South Shields it was in the name of an entirely separate new company, Arnott Newton Ltd, in order to give Robert a share in the future growth and also to protect and consolidate his position in the Group to ensure that he could not easily be ousted at a future date when I wasn't watching! A branch of Arnott Newton was later opened in Chester-le-Street and to protect other valued members of staff in a similar way, further branches were opened in the name of Arnott Thomson and Arnott Wood to give Marilyn and Les shareholdings and directorships. The companies were corporately known as The Arnott Northern Insurance Group. My instincts told me that Brooks would have to be watched if he were not to create problems. These new directors would be my eyes! I had already become aware that Brooks could be devious and ruthless but he was charming and persuasive with it. But were these not precisely some of the qualities needed to take our organisation forward quickly? Having put in place what I thought were adequate safeguards against any excesses and a generous reward structure for success, I didn't want to be constantly involved in the day to day running of what was now already a fairly substantial group of companies. I'd had twenty five years of that and it was somebody else's turn to take the pressure.

Although he should have felt threatened by Brooks, Robert Newton seemed only too willing to acknowledge him as his boss. Consequently Brooks, realising he had little choice, accepted Robert's appointment as Group General Manager and, at least in one of the companies, his co-director. This made me feel more comfortable and Brooks, who I'm sure sensed this, and with perfect timing, put it to me that I should consider appointing him as the Group Managing Director and for me to assume the position of Chairman. A Managing Director has far reaching decision making autonomy within a company and I felt a little uneasy about transferring this power to someone who I hadn't known for long and who had little knowledge or experience of the insurance business. There was no doubt in my mind that Brooks, like Ian Fletcher, a workaholic, would achieve things even though I knew that he would do so in his own way and largely for his own gratification and gain. He was hungry for power and success and had as far as I could see, few interests outside of work apart from his pet cockatoos and other exotic birds.   Provided however I and the companies were to benefit from what he may achieve by his single mindedness and drive, I persuaded myself that these need not necessarily be perceived as a threat. I wouldn't mind being a goalkeeper in a team which included a determined and tireless striker who scored lots of goals and won all our matches. Actually Brooks, who was to later achieve fame as a football club chairman, at that time certainly had no interest in the game. I don't think he had been to a match in his life.

Brooks, as I have said, could be very persuasive. I gave his proposal serious consideration and he became our Managing Director in 1989. Before agreeing to his appointment I first made him promise to keep me fully informed of what he was up to and to get more involved up front by meeting the insurance companies. He also promised to dispose of or distance himself from Edwin Davis Ltd where a conflict of interest existed. His subsequent response to these three promises was in the first case spasmodic, in the second perfunctory and the third he ignored completely, although he did spend less time at Edwin Davis due to his responsibilities elsewhere. Brooks made me promise something too.

My philosophy was then, and still is, to keep a low profile, unlike some who crave fame and publicity. Chris is the same, if not more so. In the hairdressers with Lynne Sutherland one day dressed in jeans and casual top, she gave her name as Mrs Arnott to which the girl responded, "We Arnott insured?" Chris said nothing and the girl said, "I bet you wish you were eh?" Anyway, back to my promise. I had never thought of buying a new car, preferring to let some other fool take the early depreciation. New cars for the managers, yes, but not for me. With four young children spilling drinks, dribbling ice cream, dropping crisps and discarding sweet packets I couldn't relax in a new car. My old cars usually sported metal coat hangers for aerials, the originals having become targets for vandals. I couldn't be bothered to replace them just to satisfy the destructive lust of some sad yob. This was an object of great amusement to Lynne Sutherland who would delight in pointing out to me every "managing director's aerial" she spotted. Brooks quite correctly pointed out to me that as Chairman I should improve my image because young members of staff needed to have some visible evidence of prosperity to encourage them to aspire to executive level. I kept my promise and bought a new 3.5 litre SD Rover registration number SUP 600, the very first luxury car I had ever owned.

The next few years saw us opening branches throughout the North East and in Scotland where we acquired the seven branches of Scotway Insurance Services and the two of George Weightman & Co. There was an acquisition too in Sheffield. Arngrove were busy too and Sunderland branch relocated into prestigious premises in St Thomas Street grandly named Arngrove House by Mike Graham who was generally thought to be a bit of a high flier. Arngrove House was on the corner of Frederick Street – the street in which we had over the years occupied no less than four separate buildings. Older Sunderland folk will remember it as the old Palmers department store. A separate company, Arnott (Commercial) Ltd, based in Morton House with Gerrard O'Connor as a director and shareholder, was established to deal with our commercial clients. Brooks attempted to set up a life and pensions division but his naivety and lack of insurance background and experience were exposed when it failed to live up to expectations. Brooks' appointment John Steel moved on and Sandy Shaw, a friend of mine who had joined us from Scottish Equitable did OK in Glasgow trading as Arnott Shaw Ltd but he too moved on. Ex-employees of big insurance companies with their guaranteed salaries and company cars often find it difficult to adjust to the bottom line pressures once they are exposed to the real world. Brian Sutherland on the other hand was given the Teesside client base to feed off and made a big success of his company, Brian Sutherland & Co, which was later merged into Nick Matthews' M G Shaw (UK) Ltd.

Dave Smith was no slouch when it came to drinking beer but after his marriage broke up he started drinking even heavier. He was once referred to in Lloyds Motor circles as "the fat lad from Arnotts who's always drunk", which I though was just a little unkind. Every Friday in the commercial area of Middlesbrough there was a good lunch time 'session' first at the Corner House and later at the Wig and Pen, frequented by solicitors, estate agents and mainly life assurance inspectors, plus Brian. Dave started to join them. I felt he was a bit out of his depth and had to ask him either to curtail his lunchtime drinking or, failing that, not to come back to the office afterwards where he was beginning to irritate the girls. It wasn't easy for me to do this. I liked Dave and socialised with him often, but only on evenings. It wasn't just alcohol that Dave became under the influence of. A life inspector called John Chappell persuaded him to set up business together. At that particular time certain life assurance companies apparently desperate for business were offering, before a single piece of business was placed, substantial commissions in advance in order to tie people in. Before their office door had opened Chappell Smith had spent most of this on new cars and other frivolous trappings. So many people approach business with this cart before the horse mentality. That's why so many fail. I didn't try to persuade Dave to stay with Arnotts, but I tried to give him some advice which he ignored. I suggested that they formed two companies – one to do the life assurance etc in which John Chappel would be the senior partner, and the other to do the motor and general insurance with Dave as the controlling partner. This would be his escape route. As predicted Chappell Smith didn't last long and Dave from being Motor Underwriting Superintendent at Arnotts became a counter clerk in a small local broker's office. He started to drink even more heavily than he did before and sadly died of sclerosis of the liver before he reached sixty.

While all this frantic expansion was taking place, instead of being an active Chairman and monitoring events, I left Brooks to it, a situation he was more than happy to be in. I chose a less demanding but nevertheless important role. I knew that everything depended on the Arnott client base and its annual premium income which was approaching £30 million. Without these nothing would function. Arngrove would have no properties to convert. Albany and the lawyers would have no claims to handle. There would be no-one to hire cars to. There would be no network of offices for Edwin Davis Ltd to fit out at costs approved, with a clear conflict of interests, by Brooks. Nor would there be a huge pot of money held in trust which Brooks was later to plunder to finance other ventures. However, I knew too that I controlled the client base, at least the bulk of it. This was a comfort since if it all went wrong I could sell this valuable and sought after commodity. Though nothing was said, Brooks I'm sure was well aware of this. He had to keep me sweet.

To continue our growth two things were essential. Good client service and competitive premiums. So I continued to be an ambassador for the Arnott companies since Brooks seemingly had no intention of keeping his promise in this respect. Contact with underwriters was vital in order that we retained our competitive edge. I retained some client involvement with our larger commercial customers and in dealing with complaints. Now this may seem an odd role for the Chairman of a fairly large Group to assume but I had my reasons. The number and severity of complaints are a good barometer of the efficiency of an organisation. My instructions were that any evidence of an angry or dissatisfied client must be referred to the branch manager and then to me. This way I was able to satisfy the customer that his complaint was important and was receiving attention at high level, support the staff by removing a time consuming problem from their branch and diffuse any possible action against us. I was very proud that for thirty years our Professional Negligence insurers had never been called upon to settle one single claim. I wanted to protect that record. I also knew how important it was for job satisfaction that our mostly young female staff would be able to rely on their management to help and support them. I'm sure that's why we did so well in Glasgow where our George Street office was situated right in the city centre and where there existed a higher level of abuse by customers, particularly after the pubs closed. But on the other hand our girls there were so much more streetwise and able to handle the bullies. I did have a very effective method of dealing with the worst offenders which Marilyn referred to me and it was made easy because it was Glasgow where the "F" word is part of everyday language. It may not have worked in less aggressive areas of the country. After getting the full story from Marilyn I would telephone the client and apologise. Not because we were in the wrong, because if we were we would just refund his money or compensate in some other way, but I would say I was sorry because it was true. I was sorry that we had such an obnoxious client. I would ask him to explain his problem and tell him that, even though I already had, I would look into it. "But first of all Mr McBully," I would say, "I understand that you used foul language in front of the girls in the office." They always had. Most were unrepentant. I may get a reluctant admission and half apology from others. "Well, I'm sorry Mr McBully," I would say, "but before I am prepared to take any further action I must insist that you call into the office and apologise to the girls." They never did. Bullies never do. Problem solved. Mr MacBully's file would be marked with an 'O' for obnoxious and a hefty fee slapped on his next premium. If he complained we would recommend him to insure through our main competitor so we would get rid of a nuisance and dump him on to our rival. A four pointer we used to call it. It would be a six pointer today but we couldn't get away with it because of the Data Protection Act. The COPIT client file marking system was adopted for undesirable customers. 'C' for chancer. 'O' for obnoxious. 'P' for bad payer. 'I' for idiot. The girls never told me what the 'T' stood for. Susan Wilkinson at Middlesbrough had also introduced 'Shigseye', another intriguing stratagem. There was a certain category of customer she was, to say the least, reluctant to deal with so she got all the girls to agree that when one of the category X customers came into the office, the last one to say 'Shigseye' had to deal with him.

You had to be streetwise to be at the sharp end in a busy broker's office in those predominantly customer contact, pre-telesales and pre-website days, and I found that having a mainly female staff was a distinct advantage since the majority of our customers were male motorists. The girls could handle most situations but when they needed support, I made sure they got it. In return I earned their respect. I could relate to them in a non-threatening way and they could rely on me to be understanding. Unlike a lot of males they didn't try to be too clever and they were more likely to acknowledge their limitations. I was able therefore to offer the benefit of my experience and together most problems were resolved.   In this respect they were generally less dangerous than males although we did have some very good and sensible young men on the team too. The Arnott companies were in great shape when Brooks was appointed MD.

By far the biggest source of complaints I had to deal with stemmed from motorists who told lies. Insurance is a contract "Uberimae Fides" – utmost good faith, which means that motorists must disclose on their proposal forms full details of their driving records – convictions, accidents etc and any other factor which may affect the underwriters' assessment of the risk. But by doing so they would often have to pay a higher premium. The temptation to lie, therefore, was obvious. Much of our staff training revolved round this principle. The consequence of non-disclosure would often be a declined claim and the consequences of a declined claim would usually be an angry customer. More often than not, because the client knew only too well that he was guilty, the complainant would be the overprotective spouse or parent of the dishonest policyholder. "Our Billy/my husband doesn't tell lies," they would insist. "He told the girl about the previous accident/conviction, etc." The implication being that the girl made a mistake by ignoring the disclosure and putting 'no' instead of 'yes' on the proposal form. I included in our Terms of Trading a condition that we would only discuss matters concerning our client's policy with the policyholder himself or herself – after we were caught out once when a woman cancelled her husband's car insurance after an argument in the hope that the police would stop him and charge him with driving without insurance. I think she even tipped the police off. Hell hath no fury etc!

People would often threaten us with the press who at one time would print anything for a story. Something that really irritated me once was a report in the *Newcastle Evening Chronicle* discrediting our We Arnott Insured slogan, stating that we had turned down a poor woman's claim without justification, accompanied by a photograph of a sad Mrs Liar next to her damaged car. Her husband had been driving at the time and he was banned due to a drink driving conviction. She claimed that she didn't know of his conviction when she answered 'no' to the relevant question on the proposal form. The reporter believed her. Her insurance company didn't, and nor did we. Would you? The press have too much power. They can print a totally misleading report and get away with it, damaging in the meantime a reputation which may have taken years to establish. A two-line apology in small print later does little to restore a damaged reputation.

Apart from instances like this, I really enjoyed dealing with these complaints. As I said earlier, if they are genuine then apologies and compensation are readily offered. But I didn't like the idea of deliberate liars getting away with it and being subsidised by all those honest and truthful motorists who pay the correct premiums.

As solicitors became more approachable and encouraged people to litigate, lots more complaints were put into their hands. Indeed I would encourage this since I would rather deal with a professional antagonist than someone who thinks that they will get their own way by shouting, swearing and threatening. I got a lot of satisfaction out of my encounters with the legal profession and I don't think I ever came off second best with any of them. My tactics were simple and can be summed up in one word –"attrition". I would never respond to a solicitor's letter in a confrontational way, always replying simply to request clarification on one or two points. When these were forthcoming I would ask for further clarification. Then in subsequent letters I would take a more bullish stance. I knew only too well that at some point the solicitor would ask to be 'put in funds' by his client and the more letters we wrote and the more interviews with his client were necessary then the higher would be his fee. My approach always sent out the message that we were not afraid of confrontation, that we may just have some undisclosed reliable item of defence up our sleeves and were not therefore to be intimidated by threats of litigation. Faced with mounting costs most people would drop their cases, often on the advice of the lawyer who was probably well aware that they had little or no merit. A couple of cases did end up in court. We won them both. You don't go to court unless you are pretty certain you are going to win – unless of course you do it to make a point – or three – as I did in my confrontation with the English Football Association described in Volume I.

With others taking the day-to-day pressures of running the companies I could further indulge myself in lighter matters like social occasions at Morton House and even a bit of amateur journalism. Several years earlier I had produced a public relations magazine and I resumed this practice, which was becoming fashionable within larger organisations. "In House" was our internal newsletter and *Arnott News* our PR publication which was sent to our clients and our insurers.

Such was the professional standing of Arnotts at this time, I was invited by the Department of Business Studies at a local college to give talks to their students. The title of my address "Discrimination Rules OK" captured the students' imagination, always ensured a good turn out and stimulated a lot of reaction as I attempted to explain why insurance companies 'discriminated' against and charged higher premiums for students, elderly and sometimes disabled drivers and others in high risk categories. Faced with the task of keeping their attention for an hour or so on a subject perceived to be as dull as insurance their participation made the task less daunting for me. A scary but nevertheless very satisfying experience. A group of the students which included a friend of mine, Harry Brown who became regional manager for NSPCC, approached me to do some research into Arnott Insurance and produce a dissertation as part of their study course. I readily agreed and their report

"Arnott Customers Important" earned them a distinction and contained some very pertinent observations and recommendations worthy of serious consideration. Indeed it was my intention, at an appropriate time, to implement many of them.

Drawing on my experience and with more time on my hands, I was able to produce some Terms of Trading designed for our protection which included the "no mams, dads or spouses" clause mentioned earlier. I also had plans to develop an idea I had to revolutionise Contracts of Service. I never got round to this, Harry Brown's ideas, or a number of other things which would have benefited the Company. I became cocooned to a certain extent in a self-imposed ivory tower fearful of peeping out in case I didn't like what I saw. I was vaguely aware that I would not. I didn't know, didn't want to know, how dark the clouds were which were gathering on more than one horizon.

Unlike the Emperor Nero I didn't have a fiddle and wouldn't have known how to play it if I had. Instead I buried my head in my holidays, my golf and other pleasurable social aspects of my life at that time.

Mike Graham, in characteristic grandiose fashion, announcing the official opening of Arngrove House. Also in the picture are Brooks Mileson and the Mayor of Sunderland, with a reluctant me, Ken Lee and Gerry Burge who would rather have been getting on with our jobs earning the money to pay for it.

Thirteen

BLACKMAIL

We somehow managed to keep our feet above water.
Chrissarism

I KNOW HOW THE VICTIMS of blackmail feel. They meet the blackmailer's demands hoping that will be the end of it. Then further demands are made – and further demands after that. But they can put a stop to it. They can come clean and reveal their dark secret thereby removing the blackmailer's power. Or they can go to the police. They could even shoot the blackmailer. None of these options were available to me. The ability of my syndicates to make losses was astounding. Thirty decades of profitable trading by Lloyds and I had to choose the one which went wrong! Their demands for cash calls became more frequent and the amounts more substantial. I was having difficulty paying the avalanche of cash calls made on me. My funds at Lloyds had been drawn down on and I faced bankruptcy. From a position of being in control, I then felt no longer in charge of my destiny. The last thing I needed at this critical stage in the Arnott companies' development was such a distraction and to find myself in a position of weakness. I needed to raise money. I was desperate. If I were to file for bankruptcy the repercussions on our companies would have been too horrendous to contemplate. Poised as he was to take over the reins, Brooks could not allow the liquidators to get their hands on my shares. He wouldn't be able to manipulate them as easily as he could me. Over the next few years I borrowed heavily on my director's account, which as a result became dangerously overdrawn. We set up a slush fund into which was deposited every possible bit of spare cash from the companies. Brooks was a good help during that period and I felt indebted to him, which wasn't an ideal situation. In return I suppose I countenanced a lot of the things that were to happen. But still my blackmailer was not satisfied. In desperation we carried out a series of share and asset transfers between the companies which raised some badly needed cash but diluted my control and influence over them. I stood by helplessly and witnessed the gradual erosion of the massive asset I had so patiently and laboriously built up over the previous thirty years. At a low ebb I drank more and more, which caused problems at home again. For a while I became sexually impotent which, for someone who has a high sex drive and a need for sex as a release from tension, was very worrying at the time. I don't suppose anyone really noticed how depressed I was. I did a good job of putting on a brave face. With four young children demanding her attention my wife had her own problems and I was receiving little sympathy from that quarter. The temptation to stray into the solace of the arms of another at that time was very real. Paradoxically, it was my temporary inability in the erection department which probably saved my marriage.

An inability to multi-task is largely a male characteristic, which in my case is absolutely true. We males are not good at dealing with more than one thing at a time. For example I can't even read unless I have complete peace and quiet, yet my wife Chris can work, talk, listen to music and think all at the same time. On numerous occasions in noisy pubs, restaurants or at parties when we have been in our own deep conversation she has picked up on someone else's simultaneously. This can be achieved at a range of several tables or the length of a room and she is able to retain in her mind the detail from both conversations. In contrast, for me to do it justice as I always must, it is necessary to deal with one issue at a time. What was happening within the Companies at that time should have had my full attention. Instead my mind was elsewhere and I chose to ignore certain warning signs simply because I did not have the capacity to acknowledge and take on board any extra load. There was a fear too that Chris would need me were she again to fall ill. This was more than a fear. It was almost an expectation. She had no less than fifteen operations for a variety of reasons ranging from appendix removal and ovary removal before we married to carpal tunnel surgery, hernia, hysterectomy, gall stones, disc removal, hip repair and subsequent replacement, breast lump and prolapses (twice) as well as her post-natal depression problems in the nineteen seventies – and there were more in the pipeline. She has in consequence throughout our marriage, had periods of incapacity, some related to her surgery and some not, all of which have made demands upon my time while I cared for her and kept the domestic unit ticking over. With these distractions I could not perform my duties as Chairman of the Group as effectively as I would have liked. When problems arose I buried my head in the sand hoping that those who had been given the responsibility to deal with them would do so and would act in the best interests of the shareholders (of which I was the major one) and would do so with honesty, integrity and propriety. This in fact is a legal requirement and one which I have adhered to often, as I have mentioned earlier, to my own detriment. I suppose my mother was right when she used to say "You are too soft son." But then, she was a fine one to talk!

Ultimately it was my reputation at stake and I had abdicated my influence over it.

It is true that in terms of turnover the Arnott Companies grew with Brooks as Managing Director but it was my name over the door and therefore me at whom the finger would be pointed if things went wrong. There is a wonderfully apt story about one of Napoleon's Generals. At a dinner in his honour one evening someone challenged his popularity, saying, "Tell me General, don't you think that the credit for your victories in battle should be given to your subalterns? After all it is not you but they who stand in the front line and bravely face and defeat the enemy." The General thought for a moment before replying: "I would be only too happy for them to receive all the glory – if they would be prepared to take all the blame when we are defeated."

I have provided this background in the hope that it does to some extent explain my state of mind and why I took my eye off the ball, allowing certain dangerous situations to remain unchecked and to deteriorate. We never attained plc status. Far from it – pcl more like. Perilously close to liquidation!

Fourteen

THE NEW BROOM

A new broom sweeps clean. But an old brush knows all the corners.
Anon

I WAS STAYING at our caravan on the Wild Rose Park near Appleby in Westmoreland where I was looking after Chris who was recovering from one of her operations. We weren't expecting visitors so I was surprised when a car pulled up outside and even more surprised when Brooks got out. What had brought Brooks to our caravan door? What on earth had happened? This, I thought, has to be pretty serious, so I was relieved when Brooks announced the reason for his visit, which was to tell me that he was having an affair with Gerry. Pretty tough on Brooks' wife Pauline I thought, but why would he bother travelling all that way just to tell me that? Brooks too must have been puzzled by my matter of fact reaction and it wasn't until I mentioned that Gerry Robertson, who was our longest serving girl, had once been suspected of having a brief fling with Ian Fletcher that the penny dropped. "No," Brooks corrected me, "I'm not having an affair with *that* Gerry, I'm having an affair with Gerry McArdle." This was altogether a different kettle of fish; one that could have fairly far reaching implications. Gerry McArdle was the wife of our Company solicitor and our business partner in the Albany company which owned Morton House. Brooks I suspect feared an angry reaction from me but I am not given to overreaction. I remain calm in difficult situations, deal with them philosophically and think positively. I reassured Brooks that we would just have to deal with the repercussions and sort it out when I got back to work. It wasn't a case of condoning his behaviour, but simply recognising that since the milk had already been spilled, there didn't seem much point in wasting time crying over it. We would just have to assess the problems that Brooks' philandering may have created and concentrate our attention on a damage limitation exercise, in the best interests of the companies involved. Focusing the mind in this corporate way avoided having to be dragged into the personal issues

The Albany shareholding was equally split three ways and since it was clear that Brooks and John McArdle would no longer work together for the benefit of the company and, therefore, me, I would be in a delicate piggy in the middle situation. It crossed my mind that the visit by Brooks, who was of course in his most unctuous mood, had another purpose and that was to ensure that when the crunch came I would be on his side, which of course I would. I had little choice. This was a personal matter between him and John and whilst I didn't approve of or welcome this latest development I couldn't allow myself to dwell on the moral issue or whether Brooks in the circumstances had been particularly sensible since he must have realised what commercial consequences would inevitably ensue. I was involved too deeply with Brooks in our other companies to consider any other course than to support him in our joint business affairs as I had also done some years earlier on a personal level when we sat together in Middlesbrough General Hospital waiting for the result of a touch and go operation on his wife Pauline's brain tumour which, fortunately, was a success. As it transpired, John's shares were actually held in his wife's name. Conjecture later led to speculation. Having learned how devious Brooks could be, had he deliberately set out to get his hands not on Mrs McArdle, but on her shares? Or was I being too cynical?

In the meantime, following the successful development of Linthorpe Road in Middlesbrough the newly formed Arngrove Development Company, with its name a derivative of Arnott and Graham, had an opportunity to acquire a property in Denham, Buckinghamshire. This was a substantial old house owned previously by Raymond Baxter, the very well-known BBC commentator of the time. The house, I was assured, lent itself ideally to conversion into apartments and would be a very profitable development. Mike Graham and Brooks took me down to see the house for my opinion but with no experience or knowledge of this type of development I allowed myself to be convinced that it was an opportunity not to be missed. There was, I would add, little evidence of any activity on my original concept for the Arngrove Company, although Mike took care of the existing Arnott properties which were being fitted out with brand new livery – two odd shades of a greenish colour block board which I think were acquired cheap as a job lot because visually they must have been to few people's taste. Certainly not mine. I dare say Edwin Davis Ltd put a pretty big mark up on it. Naturally the contract for the refurbishment of the offices was given to Brooks' building company! My, if somewhat grudging acceptance of the Denham development, was taken by my co directors to mean that I had given tacit approval for the Arngrove Company to be taken in a direction I had not intended. I was not given an opportunity to influence subsequent decisions. Some time later, before one of my visits to see our London underwriters, I was arranging hotel accommodation when someone asked me why I didn't stay in the London apartment. As a result of this chance remark I discovered that Arngrove had acquired, this time without my knowledge, an old Georgian terrace house in Cleveland Square, Bayswater. I also discovered that because of the high cost of converting and refurbishment (again by Edwin Davis Ltd) the apartments were proving difficult to sell because of their price. There were other developments going on too, about which I had no knowledge either. This was a far cry from my original concept on which sound basis I had agreed to the formation of the Arngrove company which was evidently too mundane for fancy pants Mike Graham whose desire for the big time took the company in a more speculative direction. But where was the money coming from? Flying high is fine. But someone has to pay for the aeroplane and the fuel!

The justification for my uneasiness was confirmed later when one day Brooks came into my office and told me that the Arngrove Company had, as I feared, overstretched itself and was in difficulties, with a serious cash flow problem which the bank had declined to underwrite. To save the company from collapse he begged me to authorise a release of money from the insurance fund which was held in trust – or at least I thought it was. I didn't want to get into the complexities of the situation and up to my eyes in problems in other areas, I couldn't handle any more bad news at that time, so I told Brooks to use his judgment in the matter in his capacity of Arnott's MD, stressing that he was obliged to act in my Company's best interests. Mike Graham later came into my office and thanked me profusely for my gesture, which had saved Arngrove from ruin and preserved his job. He promised to do everything in his power to make it up to me, including personally looking after my own property interests, in particular my Workshop Units in Monkwearmouth. In leaving the Arnott insurance fund to the discretion of Brooks I had unwittingly given him the green light to fully exploit this authority, not just to rescue Arngrove, but to use client funds for his own ambitious ends.

It was round about this time when Brooks, aware of my earlier "conversion", announced that he too had become a born again Christian. I think he was disappointed with my less than enthusiastic reaction to the news. Aware of the devious and ruthlessly ambitious nature of the man it crossed my mind that the purpose of his announcement may have been to persuade me that I could place the affairs of the companies completely in his hands in the knowledge that as a committed Christian he could be trusted implicitly. But actions speak louder than words. The legitimacy of *his* "conversion" would become apparent from his subsequent conduct. Only by that would I be convinced of his sincerity. Or was I being too cynical again?

Then well established as MD, Brooks wanted to make some changes. I didn't object to the change in our bankers from Midland (now HSBC) to Barclays but I did block his proposal to change our auditors from Torgersens with whom I had dealt for many years and who were an old established traditional firm with a strict code of practice. Brooks had his own firm of auditors which he boasted, did as they were told, but I didn't want any creative accounting in my company. On Brooks' recommendation we subsequently head hunted our new bank manager, Ron Kemp and appointed him as our company secretary.

No longer being in a position to object to any decisions by the Albany company now that Brooks had effectively control of two thirds of the shares, I had to stand by and witness what I considered to be an act of sheer horticultural vandalism. The walled garden and orchard at Morton House were flattened to make room for a new office block to relocate the Albany staff. No prizes for guessing who the builder was. Morton Mews as it was called, was quite out of character in such rural surroundings. To pay for this the ULR fee added to the premiums of the Arnott policyholders was increased.

While all this was going on Brooks mentioned to me one day that an old and mutual friend Toby White had been made redundant. Needing a replacement for John McArdle's friend Mike Burgess, who supplied the hire cars for Teesside from Ring Road Motor Co in Darlington, I suggested to Brooks that Toby may be well suited to this role and to facilitate this a company was set up, largely funded by Marshall Arnott Ltd. I was under the impression that I would have the controlling interest in White Hire Ltd under the arrangement Brooks and I had come to earlier where he would be the main shareholder in any new Scottish companies and I would have control of new English companies formed within the group. Feeling sorry for Toby White and helping him for old times' sake was something I was later to bitterly regret.

Fifteen

IN OR OUT?

You can't have your cake on both sides.
Chrissarism

IN 1993 something else happened which was to put a stop to our hopes of uninterrupted growth. Indeed it was ultimately to change the way in which many people were to buy car insurance. Direct Line started to advertise cheap car insurance on TV, available only by telephone, and our client renewal retention began to suffer as a result. We were no longer the most competitive choice on the market. Personal service had been sacrificed by Direct Line on the altar of price. Our new business figures were however standing up quite well and whilst we recognised the Direct Line competition we did to a certain extent underestimate it. After all we were still competitive and we provided professional advice and personal service too and we had seen cheap insurance companies come and go in the past. It is easy to sell cheap policies but unless the growth in policyholders is maintained forever the tail will catch up, as claims have to be paid out of inadequate premiums. I did some research and produced a booklet for the broker market entitled *Together We'll Crack It* featuring a telephone with a crack down its centre. In the booklet I analysed the threat of Direct Line and put forward ways to deal with it. First of all, I demonstrated that their premiums were in fact not simply inadequate to cover the risk, but suicidally so. I deduced therefore that this must inevitably be a short-term threat – wrongly as it turned out. Nevertheless we must, to survive, play to our strengths, one of which was the personal service aspect of insurance and I proposed that we implemented one of the recommendations, indeed the main one, contained in *"Arnott Customers Important"*, the assignment I had given to Harry Brown and his university colleagues a few years earlier. This was that each client would be allocated a dedicated member of staff who would become his or her personal advisor, thus building up a relationship between them and in consequence a personal loyalty factor. As an evolvement of the "COPIT" system introduced by the girls at Glasgow, each individual client was to be given a classification depending on how important he or she was to us and an incentive bonus would be introduced to encourage customer retention. I found that the introduction of these expedients was not possible. Why? Because of the inflexibility of the bloody computer system which was not set up to allow this to happen. Members of staff each had their own computer screen but they couldn't each have their own customers. We would just have to somehow find another way to weather the storm. We managed to replace customers lost to Direct Line with new ones, thereby maintaining with the help of inflation and premium increases due to car crime, our level of premium turnover. But it was not possible to show any significant growth in client numbers. Brooks didn't agree and, perhaps out of desperation, embarked on an expensive advertising campaign engaging a local PR firm, which he used later to promote his own personal image. Since personal recommendations accounted for most of our enquiries I had grave doubts about the effectiveness of such a campaign. We came up with some catchy jingles and messages for the radio campaign, but at the end of the day little if any increase in the number of enquiries was generated, and in any case, I argued, if our quote wasn't the cheapest then we were unlikely to get the business. In my view the main value of general advertising is name awareness. We already had that and if we needed a boost for this aspect then we should have resurrected and intensified my car sticker idea, which cost us next to nothing and was no longer being promoted aggressively. But Brooks wanted to be MD so instead of stepping in and overruling him, as I should have done, I allowed him to do things his own way. It's no good having a dog and barking yourself was the flimsy justification I used for my reluctance to act decisively. I wonder if the reason for not making full use of the car sticker idea was that he didn't think of it.

Another knee jerk reaction by Brooks to the Direct Line competition was to set up in Sunderland a separate office (with all the associated expense involved), an Arnott Direct telesales centre, which again I thought was a futile gesture since they had no better rates than the branch offices. Why, I wondered, was Brooks so desperately trying to drum up more business? This was the time, which comes to every business, for consolidation. A time to draw in the horns and live off your fat. To perhaps close or merge branches.

The first real hint of serious problems were to come to my attention in 1995 when I started to receive telephone calls from people in the business who I had known for years. Could I look at their account please? They were having difficulty in obtaining settlement and couldn't get any satisfaction from the people in the accounts department or from anyone else. I began to realise how serious the problem had become. What had happened to that twenty per cent or so of turnover, which had in the past rested comfortingly in the Arnotts bank? Incredibly, with its substantial turnover and its control of client funds, Arnotts was in a cashflow crisis and to take the heat out of the situation needed an injection of funds to get the insurance companies off our back. Brooks had clearly been feeling the pressure too. His health suffered. He had started to smoke, much to the dismay of Mike Graham who had taken it upon himself to declare Morton House a no smoking zone. So strongly did Mike feel about it, having recently lost his father from lung cancer, that he once had the audacity to make his feelings clear on this issue in his attitude to my wife who, with my approval, ignored the rule when she visited and smoked in my private office. He didn't dare say anything to Brooks though.

Had Brooks shared with me earlier the full extent of the problems we were facing I'm sure we could have worked something out together, but I needed to know exactly what had been going on and where all the money had gone and I don't think Brooks was very keen for me to find out. The calls from my friends in the insurance business were becoming more frequent and more menacing. I was deeply concerned for my reputation and that of Arnott Insurance. One of our Lloyds Brokers, Edgar Hamilton and Wellard, withdrew their guarantees and as a result we had lost the agency facilities covered by those guarantees so necessary for our competitiveness and therefore our survival. My relationship with Terry Wellard and his fellow directors, Ken Gregory and Peter Allen, had been close and convivial and the severance of our connection was deeply embarrassing all round. Rodney Boot of Holmans, our other main Lloyds guaranteeing broker, was also poised to pull the plug on us, as were several insurance companies. The dilemma was clear. We needed to show some growth in premium to keep ahead of the game but without competitive markets this couldn't be achieved. Rumours of our plight in the insurance market were rife and what that did was to create the very situation we wanted to avoid. Instead of giving us more time to settle accounts our insurers were giving us less.

I decided it was time for Brooks and I to have a lengthy talk and went up to Morton House one day resolved to do that, only to find that he had disappeared. No-one, not even Margaret Swales, his secretary in whom he confided everything, knew where he was. Margaret had made all the obvious enquiries and was concerned for him as indeed we all were. I was concerned too about the reason for his disappearance.

One of the reasons given to me by Brooks for his desire to change our auditors was that Torgersens were always slow in producing our annual accounts and I didn't pay much attention therefore when they were as much as two years overdue. With my head still buried in the sand, I had relied on Brooks and given him a free rein for too long. I needed to find out for myself what was going on. I instructed the accounts office to send along to my office all the up to date bank statements and audited accounts. When I examined the accounts I didn't like what I saw. Things like substantial payments to Edwin Davis Ltd and Albany ULR I expected, but what caused me the greatest concern were some sets of accounts, which I had never even seen. How could that be? How can the Chairman of Companies not have seen and approved their accounts? I had thought the reason I hadn't seen up to date accounts was down to Torgersen's tardiness. Not so. The accounts had been signed by Brooks – and Ron Kemp! Were things that bad that they had to keep things from me by subterfuge?

When I examined the accounts it was clear that my companies – the ones in which I had the majority shareholdings – were, from my brief investigation, in worse shape than the others. Brooks had mentioned on a few occasions how well Scotland was doing compared to England. Why, I wondered? Were my companies being stitched with Group expenses, which should have been shared out between all the companies? When a loan was needed was it always my companies that provided it? Was money from my companies used to buy the Scotway chain which was merged into and became an asset of Brooks' Scottish company? These and many other questions needed to be answered. I had said to Brooks that because of Ian Fletcher's shares in Marshall Arnott Ltd, any expansion should be concentrated on the new companies, but I hadn't intended this to be license for him to plunder its assets to *my* personal detriment too.

I am fortunate to have in Joe Laidler someone who is not only a good friend and confidante, but very wealthy too. Joe and I discussed the situation at Arnotts and he was more than willing to become involved. As the first step in our plan of action a letter was drafted by us both and sent from Laidler International to me. In that letter, among other things, Joe offered to introduce immediately an initial funding of £1 million into Marshall Arnott and the other English companies, which I controlled, in return for which he would become a director. One of the thoughts was that he would buy some of my shares and together we would get our teeth into the business of finding out where exactly the millions of pounds that should have been in the bank account had disappeared to. Having assumed again a hands-on control I would be able to tackle a number of issues about which I was unhappy, of which White Hire, which I will come to later, was but one. We would get round to it all in good time. There were a number of immediate measures we would have introduced, one being to address the enormous amount of money being unnecessarily paid to Albany ULR which I estimated at around half a million pounds a year. ULR cover by then had become freely available in most comprehensive motor insurance policies, yet the Arnott policyholders were being charged £6 each for duplicated Albany cover, often enough to make the difference between winning the business with the best quote or losing it. Many solicitors had started to offer this service free and other ULR providers were offering the same service for as little as £1 per case. The Albany coffers were overflowing at the expense of Arnotts and their customers.

Aware of the value of our client base, I also took the precaution, at the same time, of testing the market to see what price I could get for it. Swintons who were owned by the Sun Alliance Group were still looking for acquisitions although in the light of developments in the market generally the price had reduced to between one and two times of annual commission income, from twice that only a few years earlier, and bearing in mind the critical situation we were in I was not in a very good bargaining position. However the immediate problem could have been solved by a sell out in this way and I opened negotiations with Swintons in Manchester. I allowed this to be known in the market, which I know caused some insurers to delay pulling the plug on us. Brooks who had meanwhile returned to work was anxious for me not to go down the sell-out road saying that whatever we got for the goodwill would simply pay off what we owed to the insurance companies with little left over in the pot except the properties which had obviously been purchased with insurance companies money. So what? My reputation would be intact and properties are not a bad investment as Brooks himself was later to demonstrate.

The effect of Joe's letter on Brooks I can only imagine. On the surface he took it calmly and he said he could sort everything out without Joe and his money. He would come back to me with his proposals without delay. A few weeks later and true to his word he did. He had found a buyer for my shares and I would receive a lot more money for them than I could elsewhere if I would agree to the consideration being paid to me over a period of five years in equal instalments during which time I would be paid a decent salary and expenses as an independent consultant. It was tempting. But so too was the desire to find out the truth and I would have Joe to help and support me. There were signs too that there may be an easing of the pressure on me on the Lloyds scene, which for years had consumed my thoughts, damaged my confidence and dragged me down so much. Being free of this distraction would enable me to focus my mind and devote my full attention to the task that lay ahead were Joe and I to decide on that route. Once more I found myself at a commercial crossroads. Oh, if only, instead of inviting Brooks on board, I had instead turned to Joe in whom I was later to discover another business ingredient – probably the most important one – trust.

Arnott's senior staff at a reception in the ballroom at Morton House on the Group's 30th anniversary.

Sixteen

GOOD TIMES

Remember and cherish all your happy moments.
They make a fine cushion for old age.
Christopher Morley

REFLECTING ON MY FORTY-FIVE YEARS as an insurance man I was able to take some comfort. It hadn't always been stress and problems. Far from it. Insurance has given me a good life, not only financially but socially too. I met many interesting characters and I employed some too. We have insured people from all walks of life – from burglars to barristers – and they too have provided a rich source of material for the chapter entitled 'We Arnott Amused.'

Yes, there is a thriving social side to what most people perceive as a dull profession, some examples of which I have already recounted in "Morton House". The annual dinners of the Chartered Insurance Institute could be great social occasions as were the annual seminars in Majorca as guests of David Holman, one of our Lloyds Brokers. Our own Christmas parties were eagerly anticipated events and never failed to live up to their reputation – one built up over the years from the early Sunderland semi basement days. Many of our 'suppliers', both insurance companies and Lloyds brokers and underwriters held regular social events and corporate hospitality days to which I, and sometimes my senior colleagues, were frequently invited. My favourites of course were the golf outings. Hot air ballooning I found a little tedious and I couldn't get the hang of flying helicopters. Why is their steering mechanism designed for dyslexic people? Anyone who has tried to fly a helicopter will know what I'm talking about. Days at the (horse) races were always fun and I was fortunate to enjoy the corporate hospitality of General Accident at the Open Golf Championship at Sandwich and of Orion Insurance at the British Grand Prix, Silverstone.

Although I regularly attended CII Dinners all over the country, some were quite formal and I probably enjoyed most of all the ones on my doorstep. Middlesbrough Insurance Institute dispensed with much of the formality, hired a good comedian and let us get on with enjoying the company at our tables. We organised our own table at Sunderland in 1981 when I held the office of President there, an occasion on which Brian, who was one of my guests, distinguished himself by upsetting Arthur MacBeth, who he didn't know and who was our biggest competitor in Sunderland. Arthur was a flamboyant character who liked to be noticed and drove a Rolls Royce with his personal number plate of course. No wonder Tom Cowie, the local multi-millionaire businessman, set up his own insurance business, Coins & Co, in Sunderland in competition with us. Arthur's ostentatious lifestyle had clearly led Mr Cowie to assume there was a lot of money to be made from the car insurance business, particularly since he was the area's leading car sales operator. Arthur suggested that we ganged up on him and blocked his agency applications. I pointed out to Arthur that had he kept a low profile like me we wouldn't have been facing the problem in the first place.

Getting back to Brian, let me explain that the CII Dinners were always black tie and dinner jacket occasions but true to character Arthur had to be different, wearing on the occasion of my Presidency, a MacBeth tartan jacket. Brian was enjoying the occasion, particularly the wine which, despite the liberal quantity I had supplied, quickly ran out. Brian called over the wine waiter in true Glasgow "Hey you Jimmy" style and was blanked. He tried again a little later and received the same response. "The bastard wouldnae get away with that in Glasgow," announced Brian, "and he's no' going to ignore me in bloody Sunderland" – whereupon he followed the head waiter, determined to give him a bollocking. Fortunately I managed to restrain him and to explain that he was a VIP guest and not the wine waiter. "Well, why is he dressed like one?" demanded Brian when we returned to the table.

Dinners in the larger cities in which the regional offices of the major insurance companies were located and which therefore were major insurance centres, tended to be more formal occasions where examination awards were presented and serious speeches delivered – and where the behaviour of guests was, shall we say, less boisterous. There was one notable exception. Neil Cranston, a Fellow of the Institute, had left the insurance company for whom he had worked as an inspector and had set up in business as a broker in Stanley, Co Durham. At the Newcastle-upon-Tyne dinner in 1984 he was the guest of the Sun Alliance Group. So was a fellow broker, Arthur Powlett, or should I say the husband of a fellow broker. Mr Powlett had a few years earlier gone bust and taken Neil's company, Bradford Pennine Insurance, for several thousand pounds. Neil, who was the inspector responsible for Powlett's account had carried the can. Naturally he bore some resentment towards Powlett, particularly since he had been allowed to start up in business again in his wife's name and had been granted agency facilities despite his track record. Neil's indignation was inflamed by a combination of substantial participation in his hosts' wine, the sight of Powlett's affability and his hosts' obsequious behaviour towards him. By the end of the evening Neil's mood was a dark shade of black. His sense of outrage and injustice had reached boiling point. He confronted Powlett who made the mistake of treating Neil's outburst with disdain. I didn't hear what Powlett said to Neil but I, and everyone else, heard the screech of pain as he felt the full force of Neil's fist on his nose. Powlett I must say made a meal of it. He was taken out in a wheelchair to the ambulance, which had been called quite unnecessarily. Neil was subsequently summoned to appear before the CII hierarchy at their Aldermanbury HQ in London where he received only a reprimand – well worth it in return for the obvious satisfaction he had experienced from his moment of summary jurisdiction and punishment. He had literally struck a blow for justice. Good for him.

The Holman so-called Business Seminars in Palma, Majorca were, let's be honest, just an excuse for us all to have a jolly good tax deductible time – and we certainly did enjoy ourselves. They were opportunities to meet brokers from all over the UK, to play golf in the sunshine and sample Spanish cuisine and hospitality. On three of these occasions I invited colleagues to share these trips with Chris and I. We were joined first by Dave Smith, then by Iain and Pat Ferguson and later by Dennis and Lyn Mee. My wife always accompanied me with great reluctance. She was afraid that she would be out of her depth mixing with these very posh and important people from Lloyds. In fact most of the motor underwriters were just nice ordinary people, many from London's East End who, had they not been successful underwriters, could well have been successful barrow boys. I was hoping that she may gain some self-confidence by being forced to mix. At our very first gala dinner she was fortunate to be seated next to Peter Warne the senior underwriter of Milestone Motor Policies. Peter was a perfect gentleman and charming dinner companion who managed to make Chris feel relaxed – quite an achievement. He was a gastronomic connoisseur and spent the first couple of years of his retirement travelling around Europe revisiting his favourite eating houses. He also made a point of paying farewell visits to a select few of his favourite brokers. I was honoured to find Arnotts included in his itinerary. Chris, despite their earlier affinity, could not be persuaded to join Peter and I for dinner when he paid his farewell visit to the North East. I had chosen the Cleveland Tontine Bistro for our dining venue and Marilyn was only too happy to be my substitute escort. The Tontine had recently received several top restaurant awards and it would be interesting to see Peter's reaction to our region's premier restaurant. He was impressed and possibly a little surprised by the extent and quality of the menu and even more impressed when, failing to find his favourite claret on the wine list he asked, probably rhetorically, whether it was available. "Of course sir," said Christy

McCoy, the owner's brother, and much to Peter's delight produced from the cellar the precise bottle requested, after offering him the choice of several vintages. The dessert plates having been cleared away, Peter winked and said, "I'll catch him out this time." He called Christy over and ordered his very favourite vintage port and special cigar. Again the restaurant came up trumps. The three of us shared a truly gratifying eating experience. I can't describe how much satisfaction it gave me when after the meal Peter declared that this had been one of the best meals he had experienced during his forty odd years in pursuit of culinary excellence all over the world. Well done the Cleveland Tontine.

Our staff Christmas parties were occasions to say thank you to our staff and I attended them all, even when, as the company grew, we had to hold three – one for each region. They were enjoyable of course, but with everything else going on at that time of the year I was exhausted by Christmas day. For as long as possible I had organised just one party so that staff could meet and enjoy the company of colleagues from different regions but eventually it became logistically impossible. There are so many Christmas Party stories to tell and incidents to relate but I've chosen to select only two. One I will save for the next chapter – The Last Word. The other concerns a young man called Douglas who I employed at Glasgow. I was delighted that such a bright well educated young lad, instead of going to Oxford or Cambridge, had decided to choose insurance as a career and us as an employer. Such was the quality of his CV, which included an 'A' grade in French at Higher Level, that I didn't bother to check on his certificates or his references.

The 1982 party was hosted by the Teesside Region and was to be held at the Billingham Arms. For a laugh I sent a sample French menu to all the branches for the staff to make their choice of courses in advance. Below is a sample of the menu I circulated.

MENU

Crottes des Moutons
Ou
Champignons Veneneuse
Ou
Potage au Singe
xxxx
Confits des abats et asticots
Ou
Le Viande rance aux tetrads
Ou
Salade des herbes mauvaise
xxxx
Poire au sauce morveuse
Ou
Les Glaces Chaudes
Ou
Fromage moisie
xxxx
Café et alcool a bruter

The girls at George Street didn't have a clue so they passed the menu to Douglas for interpretation. Here was his opportunity to put his French 'A' grade into practice. He waffled unconvincingly and the girls soon realised he was bullshitting. He had obviously somewhat embellished his CV. He didn't understand one item on the menu either. Not surprising really. Below is the English translation.

MENU

Sheep's Droppings
Or
Poisonous Mushrooms
Or
Monkey Soup
xxxx
Conserve of Giblets and Maggots
Or
Rancid Meat with Tadpoles
Or
Puss from squeezed pimples
Or
Weed Salad
xxxx
Pears in snot sauce
Or
Hot ice cream
Or
Mouldy cheese
xxxx
Coffee and Methylated Spirit

Hadrian's wall was no deterrent to the invading Scottish troops arriving for It's a Knockout at Morton House.

Seventeen

THE LAST WORD

*As you get older you don't get more sensible, just more aware of
the consequences – until the third bottle of wine.*
Mary Millen Thomson

AS I'VE MENTIONED EARLIER those at the front end of
personal lines insurance need to be streetwise. It is not easy
dealing with people who are customers only grudgingly and who buy
insurance only because they have to. Our offices were always very
busy and our front line staff worked very hard. They also played hard.
I used to encourage this and join in whenever I had the chance. My
philosophy was that staff who play together stay together and that's
why we had a good team on and off the pitch.

After I retired I still managed to see some of the old staff from time
to time and when I was in Glasgow for the Davis Cup Tennis in 2005 I
met up with Marilyn, her daughter Fiona and Barbara McGrotty.
Barbara, before she married, used to be head of our Scottish Motor
Underwriting team and if there was ever an inappropriate name for a
girl then Barbara's was it. Slim, elegant and good looking she
deserved to be called Barbara McPretty instead. She later married
Martin Oliver a director of the Kwik Fit insurance arm and set up her
own maternity wear business.

In April the following year I again met up with Marilyn, her other
daughter Sarah and Jackie Hillis, another of our senior girls who we
had inherited from our takeover of Scotway Insurance. Again we
spent hours reminiscing over lunch and several bottles of wine. My

trip on this occasion was a sort of fact finding mission to gather some material for this book and I asked Marilyn and Jackie if they would like to send me their random observations – a bird's eye view of those happy times. Here follows an unabridged response.

MARILYN'S MEMORIES

The following are some memories from Marilyn Thomson and Jackie Hillies, originally discussed (hic!) over lunch in Café Andaluz.

After the takeover of Scotway by Arnott Insurance in June 1989 Brooks Mileson and Mairi Scott met Jackie Hillies for lunch at the Radnor Hotel in Clydebank. Their purpose was to ask Jackie to take over the Clydebank Branch as Manager when she returned from maternity leave the following month. Brooks asked Jackie if she'd be OK looking after a large branch like Clydebank after having a baby. Her reply was, "I've had a baby, not a fucking brain transplant." There was dead silence – then Brooks said, "You could be sacked for that remark." Jackie responded, "I could sue you for being sexist." There was a pause and then Brooks laughed and offered her the job. On the subject of Brooks my daughter Sarah and I attended his 50th birthday celebrations at his mansion The Hill near Carlisle, the location of, as rumour has it, rather naughty goings on. However, whilst we were there we didn't see anything untoward in that respect. The theme was to dress up in sixties gear and sixties music was blaring all night with dancing, singing, not to mention drinking unlimited amounts of booze. Sarah went off back to the hotel around 3 a.m. and I followed her about 7 a.m. although the party was still going strong with Brooks boasting that he stayed up all night drinking every week! Brooks' appearance can be quite unsettling, with his long hair, pony tail, unshaven look and his manner can be rather intimidating. Sarah said he looked like an ugly George Best.

Lookism – This is a phrase the Arnott girls used to describe their tendency to criticise customers' and others' looks and appearance – e.g. "She's an ugly fat cow, isn't she?"

To go back to the meeting Jackie had with Brooks whilst she was on maternity leave, she (like me when first dealing with him on the telephone) got his name mixed up. Both of us kept calling him Miles Brookson instead of Brooks Mileson. At the meeting with him and Mairi she mentioned this, saying, "What kind of name is that anyway?" Brooks' response, "Every jug has a handle," was countered with "Most mugs have too."

In the early days in George Street (circa 1978/79) there were only two of us in the branch, Bill Farquharson and me. One Friday (being the day I always dressed up to go out after work for a night out) I thought I looked particularly fetching in a white blouse, red and white striped flared skirt and four inch sling back red sandals. This particular Friday a customer came in for his Green Card, which he had been promised, but which had not come in that day's post. The customer was insured with Eagle Star who had offices about ¾ mile uphill from George Street so Bill told me to go and get the Green Card from their offices for the customer. He told me to hail a taxi in the street, knowing full well that a taxi for hire in the city centre on a Friday afternoon could not be had for love or money. So, I walked to the Eagle Star offices in these far from comfortable shoes and collected the aforesaid Green Card. The Eagle Star offices were situated in Blythswood Square which at that time was part of the red light district of Glasgow but in my innocence I didn't think this would be a problem since it was early afternoon on a bright and sunny summer's day. Was I wrong! A gentleman (?) approached me and asked, "Do you have the time?" Stupidly I misunderstood and looking at my watch, told him the correct time of approximately 2 p.m. "No, no," he said, looking me up and down in what I can only describe as a leering and very creepy way. "You know what I mean" – this was accompanied by a wink. I turned bright red, told him to fuck off and marched off in as dignified a manner as I could. I didn't look back. By the time I arrived back at the office my feet were killing me and had swollen up so much I had to take off my gorgeous shoes to go back and forward to the counter to serve customers. Bill Farquharson found the whole story hilarious and whilst I laughed with him inside I was seething. You see, I had asked him if I could phone and book a taxi to take me to and from the Eagle Star offices and he had refused, saying I could hail one easily outside. This of course was not the case. Not one taxi for hire passed me either way. That night I was out with my pal Irene and our two boyfriends of the time, John and Bob. My feet were throbbing, that is until I had consumed enough booze to deaden the pain. We all stayed over at Bob's flat that night and I needed little egging on not to go into work on the Saturday morning. I was supposed to be working with Bill from 9.15 a.m. until noon. Feeling extremely hard done by (he thought nothing of leaving me on my own for hours at a time while he went to the pub during working hours) I allowed Irene to phone to ask for me. He said, "She was going out with you last night and hasn't turned in for work – don't you know where she is?" Irene, being a world class liar, said I had gone home early because I was upset at being propositioned the day before and also that my feet had swollen up to twice their normal size. Believe it or not he swallowed it. When I turned up for work on the Monday morning he was so solicitous of my welfare I almost felt guilty. Almost.

Some years later, circa 1985/86, Derrick and Brian (Sutherland) visited George Street and after the office closed we all repaired to the Georgic pub next door for a drink. At least that's what I told my partner John Ferguson when I phoned home to say I would be a little late. Well, one drink led to another, to another and so on and several hours later we were all up for going for a curry. I phoned home again to be given the cold shoulder routine. When I returned to the table I said to Derrick and Brian, "God you two might talk about being henpecked, but I'm cockpecked." I can't remember if we did go for that curry but I seem to remember that John realised the number of times he'd pulled the same stunt far outnumbered my falls from grace. The boot was merely on the other foot!

During the eighties we had a lot of fun socialising with the locals in the Dunrobin and the Press Bar. A typical crowd drinking together could easily include John & Lawrence Jamieson, local shopkeepers,

Jimmy Martin, a local garage owner, Lecturers from Strathclyde University (of which my partner at the time John Ferguson was one), journalists from the *Glasgow Herald* and *Evening Times*, the Deputy Governor of Barlinnie, Jimmy Stewart (affectionately known as 'the gay guv'), Jimmy the Porn who worked for British Telecom (BT offices were a few doors down from us) and who earned his nickname because of his well-known liking for saucy magazines and blue movies. Also present at any given time at one of these gatherings could be Jimmy the Poof, a lovely guy who had at one time been a male prostitute in London and who was in and out of gaol for soliciting, breach of the peace, etc. The list is not exhaustive and of course I have to include myself and the girls from George Street, the two Eileens, Barbara and the girls from Beneficial Finance who could, believe it or not, even outdrink us. I'll never forget the night when Margaret Jamieson, John & Lawrence's mother, and Father Murphy, the University Chaplain, both steaming drunk, gave a rendition of "A Bicycle Built for Two", Father Murphy with his trouser legs rolled up and Margaret with her skirt tucked into her knickers! Happy days.

In those days, we quite often used to party all night on the Friday and go into work on the Saturday morning still under the influence. Come Monday morning we could figure out how good a time we had had on the Friday night by the state of the writing on the copies in the cover note books!!!!! We always got away with it then but I dread to think what would happen nowadays if such behaviour manifested itself. Instant dismissal no doubt. Funnily enough, we seemed to do particularly well income wise on these Saturdays so we must have been doing something right.

After the takeover of Scotway in 1989 Derrick Arnott instigated a new annual summer event – 'It's An Arnott Knockout' – this was to enable all the staff from both England and Scotland to get together at Morton House for daytime outdoor organised sports type events (sack race, etc) and a disco in the evening indoors. The first of these was organised by a Committee headed by Robert Newton. Robert was responsible for ordering all the booze for the bar and in his opinion he had provided from the cash n' carry ample supplies of vodka. Well, at that time vodka was the 'in' drink for the Glasgow girls and since there were fifty of them supplies had run out within an hour of the bar opening. I was reported as saying to him "For God's sake Robert, where is the vodka? I'm gasping for a drink!" Poor Robert had to go to the local off sales and buy their entire stock of Smirnoff Vodka. Bless him.

Needless to say, the following year he did not make the same mistake. All the Glasgow contingent were booked into the local hostelry, the Chilton, and after the disco finished a crowd of the girls (well and truly plastered) made their way back through a back lane shortcut to the Chilton. They were singing the usual songs 'I belang tae Glesca' etc. when they were drowned out by the sound of dogs barking. Silence fell and then a man shouted at us to shut up – we were alarming the dogs. The response to this as far as can be remembered was along the lines of "Go away and shag yer dug!" Fortunately he did not appear to understand the accents but that did not stop him from complaining about us. Can't remember the outcome of that but I don't think there were any repercussions.

Mairi Scott, the daughter of Richard (Dick!) Scott, was a thoroughly spoiled and not very likeable person who, when she didn't get her own way, made everyone's life a misery. She was known by several nicknames, e.g. Cruella de Ville (the baddy from 101 Dalmations), Snake Eyes, The She Devil (due to the warts on her face!) – Lookism again! At lunch recently we added another to the list 'Nanny McPhee', after the part played by Emma Thompson in the film of the same name.

Several years prior to the takeover Mairi had gotten married. Her husband was several years younger and when they met had been in the Marines. Rumour had it that her father supplied the money to 'buy' him out of the Marines and he was given a job with Scotway. Eileen O'Donnell always maintained that the only way she got a husband was because daddy bought her one! Anyway the marriage didn't last more than a couple of years despite the lavish wedding which had been laid on by daddy. Mummy, Wilma Scott, a lovely lady with unfortunately a well-known drink problem (no wonder, it has been said, with a husband and daughter like them) wore a beautiful designer outfit and an expensively coiffed wig. At the reception she was surreptitiously getting well and truly smashed and was standing with a group of Scotway staff swaying to and fro, with a fag (in a posh cigarette holder of course) in her hand and with this held up and waving about she alas didn't notice that her wig was starting to smoulder. Only quick thinking (i.e. glass of water) prevented disaster. Poor Wilma. She and Dick split up after 40 years of marriage and I have heard that she is now the life and soul of the local bowling club with a wide circle of friends and an active social life. Good for her.

One of the staff in the Clydebank Office, Ina, 'no nonsense say it as it is' type, used to drive Jackie to distraction. All year round she wore the same duffel coat. From Autumn to Spring she wore the same pair of battered boots to work every day and from Spring to Autumn the same pair of battered beach sandals. She never wore make up, her hair always looked as if it needed a good brush and Jackie says her feet stank. However, when Ina was dressed up for a night out she was a real stunner – a Liz Taylor look-alike. I remember the first time I met her on a night out in town – I didn't recognise her – talk about glamorous. Her son worked on cruise liners and provided her with an expensive wardrobe to go on cruises every couple of years all expenses paid. (An aside here – one of the other Clydebank part-timers was mother to one of the Wet Wet Wet band – can't remember which one – will check with Jackie.) Anyway, back to Ina, she was serving a customer at the counter one day and the customer was hopping backwards and forwards from one foot to the other, obviously needing the loo. Ina was notoriously slow and was taking ages to write this cover note. The customer said, "Please hurry up, can't you go any faster, I need that cover note." Ina replied, in her own inimitable way, "Sir, I think you are in more need of a shite than a cover note."

Back on the subject of nicknames, one person who did not endear himself to the staff was Mike Graham. Jackie and I privately thought of him and the Edwin Davis crowd as 'parasites'. We reckoned they milked the company for work done on the branches. Mike was known as 'the ginger action man' because of his red hair and his propensity for making a meal out of every single item required for the branch. In particular he drove Jackie bonkers because he used to waste so much of her time (as Regional Manager) sorting out branch requirements. She was frequently heard to mutter "Money for old rope" when Mike or Edwin Davis were involved in anything.

The first Xmas after the Scotway takeover it was decided to have a Xmas Dinner at the Hospitality Inn in Glasgow for the Scottish crowd, approximately 50/60 staff and management. At that time the ratio was approximately 95% female. The cost of £25 per head was to be paid by the Directors and they also agreed to pay for one round of drinks. Well, I'm not calling the Arnott girls lushes but the thought of having to pay hotel prices for booze was not going down well since the whole object of a night out for them was to get totally pissed. A cunning plan was formed. Cases of Perrier water were purchased and drunk and then bottles washed out and filled with vodka. Each girl took one bottle in her handbag into the hotel. Jugs of soft drinks and glasses were ordered and the waiters, who knew exactly what was going on and found it hilarious, were well tipped to aid and abet us. A brilliant night was had by all! I'll leave it to you Derrick to tell the story of the whisky and vodka chaser!

End

Thanks girls. I am surprised that there was no mention of your company car, Marilyn – nor of Aphrodite's!

When Marilyn was promoted to a regional role she was persuaded, reluctantly I might add, to have a company car. First she had to pass her driving test which, given Marilyn's confidence, I assumed would be a formality. Alas, she was not a "natural" when it came to driving but she eventually managed to satisfy the examiner and obtain her license (I think she must have been wearing her Blytheswood Square outfit for the test!). During her first year of driving her white Vauxhall Astra she had no less than eight bumps, none of which were reported to me and all of them fixed as a favour by "Wee" Alex MacDonald, one of our recommended repairers. She would often freeze at the thought of driving her car and on more than one occasion I had to suggest leaving the car and getting a taxi. We are all confident in certain areas and lack confidence, often surprisingly, in others.

Aphrodite was the name given to a blow up rubber sex doll presented by the girls at George Street branch to Sandy Shaw shortly after he went there to develop the Financial Services potential which existed within our customer base. There was a suspicion that Sandy's interest in Aphrodite may have been a little more than light-heartedly platonic when he decided to take her home – dressed in the Arnott girls uniform – sussies and all! Well, we all enjoy a bit of fantasising now and again!

Now to the tale of the "voddies". We had recently taken over the Scotway chain of offices and the night in question was the occasion of the first combined Glasgow Christmas party. This was my first opportunity to meet many of their staff and I hadn't yet got the strength of them so I couldn't let my hair down as I had at previous Arnott parties. Besides, I was seated at the head of the table with Mairi and her father who, I must say, I found quite pleasant company despite him being a "Wee Free" (a strictly tea total Scottish Presbyterian). So, when the festivities came to an end at around 2 a.m. and all but the hard core of Marilyn, Barbara and Eileen Reid had left, I was in need of a drink and ordered drinks for myself and the girls from the night porter. I forgot to order a mixer for my whisky so I topped it up with Perrier Water from one of the bottles which were lying around in abundance. After my second whisky and mixer my legs refused to function and I was incapable of coherent speech despite the liberal amount of mixer I had added to these and even more liberally to my third. When I woke up the following morning I was completely wrecked. I felt I could have flown back to England without the aeroplane. I had of course been drinking a potent cocktail of whisky with vodka leftovers masquerading as Perrier Water!

Well, this is a first. This Chapter was to be devoted to the females and I've managed to get in the last word! But the final Chapter of my involvement with Arnotts and Albany had not been written. Perhaps it was too much to expect that my Agreement with Brooks could turn out to be straightforward.

One of the Glasgow Region teams (We Arnott English) celebrating victory in "It's a Knockout." Captain Marilyn is third from left.

Eighteen

THE AFTERMATH

Verbal agreements are not worth the paper they're written on.
Samuel Goldwyn

I WAS VERY DISAPPOINTED and angry when I discovered the extent to which my generosity and willingness to give Brooks so much power had been taken advantage of. I had never in the past avoided confrontation in the face of injustice as those who have read *Social Domestic & Pleasure* will know. But I was sixty years old and my battle with Lloyds had knocked much of the fight out of me. I thought long and hard about the situation in which I found myself. I knew that Brooks was devious and ruthlessly ambitious. I knew that had I been around to control his excesses then we would not have found ourselves in such a mess. I was Chairman of the Group and it was my duty to do so. I knew also that I had neglected that duty and therefore must shoulder some of the blame. Joe was up for the fight but I wasn't sure that I was. I would wait and see what proposition Brooks would put to me.

Apparently a South African company called Capricorn was interested in acquisitions and an offer for my shares was made. We drew up Heads of Terms – a list of benefits I would receive in addition to the payment for my shares. The shares of a subsidiary car hire company, White Hire Ltd were not to be included in the sale and I was to be offered Brooks' shares at 1966 market value. The 1995 balance sheet value of that company was only £32,000 despite £41,000 having been taken out of my company Marshall Arnott Ltd to set it up only a couple of years earlier. Brooks tried to dissuade me from insisting on this condition, but I had my reasons and I suspect Brooks had an inkling as to what they were. Actually had Brooks kept to our agreement on the English companies it wouldn't have been necessary for me to buy these shares at all since I would have controlled sixty per cent of the company anyway. Instead he had set up White Hire with only forty per cent of the shares in my name. But that's just another example of my failure to get involved in the nitty-gritty of what was going on.

On this basis and subject to my pension fund being transferred into a new company I was setting up, I accepted the Capricorn offer and appointed McKenzie Bell Solicitors of Sunderland to act for me.

My brother-in-law Phillip Marshall was running the Tyne and Wear depot of the car hire company into which his own business had been amalgamated. I didn't see much of him but I was aware of some friction between him and Toby White caused by certain things which Toby had done and said. It was for this reason and to protect Phillip's position that I was keen to acquire full control of White Hire Ltd and find out exactly what was going on.

On the 29th April 1997 I received an urgent telephone call from Brooks. He had finalised the deal with Capricorn, a South African company and a share sale agreement had been drawn up. He told me that Capricorn were insisting that the agreement was signed on 1st May otherwise they may pull out. Since I was in Tenerife at the time, just hours away from taking a ferry to the island of La Gomera where we were to celebrate my wife's fiftieth birthday with friends at the Hotel Mirador, it was impossible for me to be at the offices of Watson Burton, Solicitors, in Newcastle, as required. I did get a flight back to the UK as quickly as possible and the meeting was re-arranged for the 3rd May. Brooks explained that although the agreement didn't include everything we had agreed (the White Hire shares for example) it had been kept fairly simple for the benefit of Capricorn who he was anxious to keep sweet and understandably so because if this deal fell through then Arnotts, then in desperate need of funds, may have fallen through too. The main points of the deal were in the agreement and Brooks assured me that I could trust him to honour everything else we had agreed. After a brief perusal of the agreement we signed on the dotted line. At that point I became a cash millionaire and my insurance career was at an end. The consideration for my shares came to me free of tax. I also had a substantial pension fund to ensure that I and my family would be financially secure for the rest of my life. We flew back to Tenerife with a load off our minds. Brooks and I shook hands and despite everything we parted on good terms. As I have said earlier, almost everyone in business is motivated by self-interest and Brooks was certainly no exception. This is something which I may not admire but being a realist I understand and accept it, even though Brooks had taken advantage of my apathy and trust and brought my company to the brink of financial disaster. What happened next was to sour our relationship permanently. We fell out over a relatively trivial matter. The difference was that the incident or series of incidents I am about to relate affected me and my family personally rather than corporately and for this reason I found them unacceptable and unforgivable. I will try to recall the details as accurately and as briefly as possible.

Whilst I was Chairman of Arnotts my sons had the use of company cars and this was no longer possible. I would get round to buying a couple of runabouts as soon as I got time. They pestered me as young people do with their parents and they suggested that perhaps Uncle Phil might have a spare car available. He did. In fact he said he had several and that we could have two on loan, the two that were least likely to be needed. I said I would arrange insurance with Gerrard O'Connor of Arnott Commercial Limited who handled all my personal insurances but Phillip offered to do this on my behalf. All perfectly innocent you might think. Gerrard chose to include the cars in the block policy which existed and which would cover us.

A couple of days later all hell broke loose. Brooks, I am told, stormed into Gerrard's office in a rage and ordered him to take the cars off cover immediately because I was no longer a part of the company.

Apparently Toby White had passed our house and seen one of the cars parked outside and obviously had informed Brooks. I received a call from Gerrard to say the boys were no longer insured to drive them. They were using the cars at the time and had they been stopped by the police would presumably now have convictions on their licenses. I spoke to Toby White and asked him why there was a problem and it boiled down to the fact that I should have asked him and not his depot manager. Isn't it odd that such a fuss was made over the insurance issue? What Toby was saying in effect was that this wasn't the issue at all. The cars were in fact covered under the block policy, as I knew perfectly well they were, unless of course someone specifically excluded them as Brooks did. So what *was* all the fuss about? What was it about some people to whom I showed nothing but generosity, that made them appear to resent me? I do know that, even when *he* was managing the companies, it irritated Brooks that it was me that the staff held in high esteem and it was me that they acknowledged as their boss. Was it because of this, or that he considered himself superior to me and could not understand why someone so low profile as me could command more respect than him that he wanted to demonstrate his authority so forcefully? Was he another one with Fletcher's syndrome?

I was later to learn the reasons for the animosity between Phillip and Toby. Phillip had lost his temper with Toby and accused him of disgusting behaviour. Toby was looking for ways to dismiss him. I am not condoning Phillip's behaviour on this occasion but when he explained the background I understood how he felt because I felt angry too. Phillip told me of a number of things connected with the running of the business which I strongly disapproved of. He told me also of several incidents which demonstrated Toby White 's attitude towards me and my family. On one occasion Phillip mentioned to Toby that he was picking me up from Newcastle Airport and was waiting for a call from me. Toby's response was: "Well, if he hasn't phoned you before now that's his problem, isn't it?" On another occasion Phillip, whilst hers was being serviced by the local Ford dealer, had loaned Chris a car (not asking permission or insurance problems on that occasion!). Toby clearly wasn't suited. He asked Phillip why she hadn't got a courtesy car from the Ford dealer and he told him that if a car was needed for hire he would have to take that car from her. When my son James was at University in Newcastle, he offered his services for hire car delivery to earn some extra money. Toby refused and gave the job to Bill, a friend of his. Yet his daughter was given a job in my Middlesbrough branch! Now this is the man, remember, who was given a job by me when he was made redundant. The man who was gifted a twenty per cent share in the new car hire company. The man who was paid his salary courtesy of customers supplied by Marshall Arnott Limited, which had given White Hire a substantial interest free loan to get it off the ground. I am not looking for gratitude. That would be too much to expect of this sort of person, but his attitude suggested that I could be excused for thinking that he inexplicably harboured some kind of grudge against me, bordering on hatred. Perhaps he too was suffering from Fletcher's syndrome.

A couple of years after setting up White Hire a mutual acquaintance, clearly unaware of my involvement, was telling me what a successful businessman Toby had become so soon after being made redundant. Toby had obviously led him to believe that the "success" of White Hire was down to his own enterprise. There are certain people who do little to deserve or earn their positions of authority, yet cannot resist strutting their importance to others. Distasteful though this may be, I can understand how important it is for such people to demonstrate their status. What sickens me is that in their desire to be seen to be successful they forget who handed to them on a plate the opportunity. Worse than that was Toby White 's obvious and undeserved ill feeling towards me. Perhaps he may have been resentful of my success. Those who start from nothing and achieve success in business by their own sacrifice and endeavours have no need to boast about it. Upstarts do.

I didn't proceed with my acquisition of White Hire. They made it difficult for me. They would not agree to audited completion accounts, nor to the usual warranties one expects and which are standard in this type of transaction. They insisted on the immediate repayment of the £41,000 loan owed by White Hire to Marshall Arnott Ltd. They also wanted to increase the price to reflect the 1997 accounts and who knows what tinkering may have taken place before *they* were produced. I suspect that Brooks was well aware of what I would do with Toby White if I got control. I'm sure he was protecting his friend. They were members of the same Masonic Lodge. So much for Masonic principles.

As soon as I was out of the way, Phillip was sacked, ostensibly for allowing me to borrow two cars without hire agreements (which hadn't been considered necessary on previous occasions) and without insurance, which was nonsense. They had manufactured a case for dismissal. I warned Brooks that a case for wrongful dismissal was likely to result in an Industrial Tribunal. He said that White Hire would welcome this wholeheartedly. They had many issues they would like to air in court. We would see.

The Industrial Tribunal was convened on 4th November 1997. Phillip engaged as his lawyer a bitter enemy of Brooks – no other than John McArdle. Phillip's interview with Toby White at which he was dismissed, had been secretly recorded on tape and was brought to the Tribunal with a full transcript. Evidence had been obtained of certain things which had been done by the company which may not have been in the best interests of its shareholders. I was aware of these and had intended to use them when I took over White Hire. This evidence was to be put to the Tribunal suggesting that the real reason for Phillip's dismissal had nothing to do with a spurious technical matter but the fact that Phillip knew too much. I was there to give evidence on the insurance aspect. I had double-checked to make sure that the insurance had been in order. Whether or not it had been placed on the most suitable policy, White Hire's or Arnott's, was irrelevant. The broker, Arnott Commercial had been given the facts and they had arranged cover as they thought appropriate. The bullshit Brooks gave me about things having to be done differently now that they were a part of an

International Group was nonsense too. Arnott Commercial was an independent company which was not taken over by the new people.

Brooks, Toby and his brother Peter had turned up at the Tribunal full of bravado, then bottled out when it came to the crunch. Phillip was awarded, I believe, several thousand pounds in damages.

This was not to be the final occasion in which Brooks and I were to be involved in court proceedings.

Nineteen

THE KING AND I

In this life he laughs longest who laughs last.
John Masefield

WHAT WITH MY FIRST WIFE, Jack Reed, Ian Fletcher, Mike Graham, Messrs Walker (Syndicate 290), Donne (733), Judd (164), Matson (104), Fagan (540) and most of my other Lloyds Syndicate underwriters, Toby White and finally Brooks Mileson, I was beginning to feel like one of the characters in the Tale of the Constipated King, which I will now relate for the benefit of those who have not heard it before.

Many years ago in a far off and pleasant land everyone was happy except the King and one of his subjects, whose identity will be revealed at the end of the tale. The King lived in a luxurious palace, was loved by his loyal subjects and had a beautiful daughter, the Princess, but alas he suffered from a terrible affliction – constipation – from which he could get no relief despite all the advice, treatment and potions supplied by the Kingdom's leading physicians. In desperation a proclamation was issued from the royal palace in which the King decreed that whoever could find a cure would be given half of his Kingdom and his daughter's hand in marriage. Long queues formed outside the palace and hundreds of cures were offered – each one quite ineffective. The last person in the queue was a shabby nondescript youth, who the King was about to dismiss. How, he thought, could a poor young peasant help where so many wise and educated men had failed? But, by now quite desperate and despondent, he could not ignore the challenge thrown down by the lad. "Sire," he called out, "I can guarantee a cure for your torment. If I fail you may chop off my head." Intrigued by the youth's boldness the King decided to grant him his opportunity. "Follow me," bade the youth with great authority in his voice and set off across the hills and into the valley beyond. Exhausted, the King was on the verge of losing his patience when the youth pointed to a remote cottage. "There lies your destination Sire," he announced, "and there will you find the secret which will put an end to your suffering." In the courtyard of the cottage there was a well and the King was instructed to remove his breeches and place his bottom over the edge of the well, whereupon his bowels instantly disgorged their hitherto reticent contents.

What rejoicing there was in the Kingdom! The youth's old clothes were replaced with splendid finery and he was transformed into a handsome consort for the Princess. Each morning thereafter he would accompany the King on his journey across the hills to the well and one day, curious to find out the well's secret laxative power, the King asked his new Prince to reveal it. "Ah," said the Prince, "down at the bottom of the well there lives a man called Derrick Arnott – and everybody shits on him!"

I'm not bitter really. Well, perhaps a tiny bit.

Twenty

BROOKS MILESON R.I.P.

Money hasn't changed me. I still have my feet on the ground.
I just wear more expensive shoes now.
Oprah Winfrey

I **HADN'T HEARD** of Helphire plc until my lawyer wrote to
Albany Group Holdings about the money they owed me and they
(Helphire) replied. It appears that Brooks must have sold his shares to
them.

£25,000 plus VAT had been deducted from the 1999 instalment of
my Albany and Arnotts share sale settlement. I wrote to them at the
time challenging this deduction and received a reply from Bob
Jefferson the Financial Director of Albany Holdings explaining that
this was for work done by Mike Graham in managing my workshop
units and in connection with their sale in 1997. Presumably Brooks,
because he didn't want to give me reasons to pull out of the Arnotts
share sale and possibly bring Joe Laidler on board, no mention of this
"debt" had been made earlier and no provision for it had been made in
the agreement drawn up by Brooks' lawyers and checked out by mine.
In fact, the contract contained a severe penalty clause if the instalments
were not paid in full and on time. They were thus in breach of this
clause. I wrote to them pointing this out. Jefferson replied attempting
to justify the deduction. I offered to compromise. Jefferson again
replied saying that he had spoken to the Chairman (Brooks) and that a
compromise would not be considered and that as far as the Chairman
was concerned he considered the matter closed. Now it's just this sort

of arrogant attitude that gets up my nose. Arnotts had been a gravy train for which for many years Messrs Mileson and Graham and others had been given first class tickets. Brooks had got away with all but destroying my company. He wasn't going to get away with this. I wrote again warning them that I may have to consider taking further action but I kept the threat low key, not wishing to rock the boat at that point with two instalments of my settlement still due. I could be patient. The contract had been written under seal which meant that the normal six years limitation for enforcement did not apply and if and when I did get settlement it would come with interest at a juicy four per cent above bank rate.

My lawyer's letter to Helphire had obviously come as a bit of a shock to them. Brooks, when selling his shares to them had undoubtedly declared that he knew of no outstanding liabilities. He had obviously disregarded my earlier warning. This meant that ultimately it would be he and not Helphire who would have to foot the bill should my claim succeed against the plc Company who would then insist on reimbursement from him.

The case was listed for a summary jurisdiction hearing in August 2006. An adjournment was requested and granted with the defendants picking up all the costs. One of the reasons for the adjournment I learnt, was that Brooks was seriously ill in hospital recovering from a bowel operation. This didn't surprise me, or anyone else for that matter, since he publicly and apparently proudly, claimed that he lived on Lucozade and a hundred cigarettes a day.

He had been in the news a lot since 1998. Shortly after my own high profile run in with the English Football Association[2] over their draconian punishment of Middlesbrough FC resulting in the club's relegation from the Premier League, Brooks featured in a story in the *Sunderland Echo* about his possible takeover of Sunderland FC. OK, he had I'm sure plundered Arnotts but nowhere in my opinion could he have found the money for such a bold acquisition. It did more than

---

[2] 'See Volume I – DA versus FA.'

cross my mind that he may just have been a little peeved that I was getting so much publicity and was seeking a bit of attention for himself. Though why on earth he should want to do so is an anathema to me. The difference was that my action was taken for reasons of genuine outrage and I was not comfortable with the resultant publicity. Brooks, it seems, thrived on it.

He was later connected with Scarborough FC and was reported to be their Chairman for a while. But he hit the jackpot when he took over at Gretna FC who were members of the Northern League. For many years Arnotts had sponsored local minor league football clubs and when Brooks was appointed Managing Director he continued this support. The first clubs to receive our sponsorship were Marske United and Whitby Town who were also in the Northern League and later Arnotts sponsored the league itself. This was how the connection with Gretna was made and the connection was consolidated when Brooks bought a house near Carlisle and moved there. I don't know how he managed to get Gretna into the Scottish league, but I do know that there were and still are some angry Clydebank supporters whose club had to make way for them. But credit where credit's due. Gretna FC's is an, albeit brief, fairy tale success story. Their first season in the Scottish League saw them gain promotion into Division Two and the following season (2005 – 2006) they were promoted to Division One and reached the Scottish Cup Final. Though beaten in the final by Hearts they actually qualified for Europe and played in the EUFA Cup. Brooks was no doubt well pleased with all the publicity and adulation which he, I have to say, deservedly received and which it seems to me he had always craved. I don't think he felt the same when it all went pear shaped.

Brooks was reported to have sold his shares in the Arnott and Albany companies for a figure in excess of sixty million pounds – an intelligence I took with a pinch of salt since, as far as I could see, much of the shareholding in the organisation in 1997 was transferred not to him but to Capricorn, the South African company. Only a few years later he was reported to be deep in debt.

The eventual outcome of our court case was that I was awarded the £25,000 plus VAT, plus interest and was given leave to pursue an action for further substantial interest due under our agreement. My patience was well rewarded since at the time of the short payment of my 1999 instalment, there was still a substantial balance due to me and interest on this was, as I said, four per cent over bank rate. This subsequent claim was settled out of court, but due to a confidentiality agreement I agreed to sign I cannot disclose details of the settlement. From what I hear, I got in just in time. Brooks' other creditors were not so lucky.

Before embarking on this litigation Mike Graham had assured me that, because he was disillusioned with Brooks' treatment of him, their relationship had soured and he would not support his defence. He spoke with forked tongue. In fact, at Brooks' request, he did a lengthy report detailing all the work he had done on my behalf, which in fact proved quite irrelevant to the case. So much for the promise he had made to me all those years ago when I authorised the release of funds from the Marshall Arnott insurance account which rescued the Arngrove company and saved his job.

My scepticism about the size of Brooks' fortune was confirmed when I was told about an incident which I believe occurred shortly after his alleged bonanza and which to me was an indication of his state of mind at that time. He telephoned Gerrard O'Connor demanding money from Gerrard's company Arnott (Commercial) Ltd in which Brooks had retained a shareholding. Apparently when Gerrard refused his demands Brooks flew into a rage and warned Gerrard that he was on his way down to his office threatening violence if the money wasn't handed over. Gerrard refused to let him into his office and there was a confrontation in the car park. Brooks backed down. It seemed strange to me that one of Britain's wealthiest men should need to demean himself in such a manner.

"This club is my soul. I would have ended up croaking if I had not come to Gretna," famously remarked Brooks shortly after he became Chairman of the club. Not famous last words exactly but some six years later on the third of November 2008, my friend Brian Sutherland received a text from Mike Graham: "Brooks dead. Found in pond." Brian telephoned Mike to ask him what the punch line was. But Mike wasn't joking. He had been told by Brooks' brother that Brooks had indeed been found dead in a pond in the garden of his house. The story which had been released to the press was that Brooks had died in hospital after suffering a heart attack. The discrepancy in the two stories was odd. I was inclined to believe the first version. Rumours were rife that Brooks was in serious financial difficulties and had, a few days earlier, lost a battle in court led by his wife's ex-husband, solicitor John McArdle, and had been ordered to pay £1.7 million pounds.

This enigmatic character's death at the age of sixty came as no surprise to me. Brooks killed himself, as many do, in the frantic and futile pursuit of fame and fortune. My sympathy goes to his family and especially to his sons Paul and Craig who, according to their mother Pauline, saw very little of Brooks when they were young. She told me that once when Brooks came home one day, in a sardonic gesture, she lined them up at the door and formally introduced them to their father!

Gretna Football Club had failed to save Brooks from croaking. It was liquidated in 2008 and Brooks was later reported to have died with debts approaching ten million pounds – including two million owed to the club.

Brooks Mileson was declared bankrupt sixteen months after his death. Only two million of his alleged fortune could be accounted for. His creditors, assuming that the rest of it had been cleverly secreted away somewhere, undertook a costly worldwide investigation into its whereabouts. I could have saved them the bother. Kowing the man and having some inside knowledge of the Albany and Arnott businesses before I sold out, my guess is that the reported £60 million paid to Brooks when *he* sold out was wildly exaggerated by him in order to boost his extraordinary ego.

Twenty One

WHAT NEXT?

I don't think anyone should write their autobiography until they are dead.
Samuel Goldwyn

WHEN I PHYSICALLY RETIRED at the age of sixty-one my mind didn't follow suit. The first thing I did was to set up a new company, Teesdale Trading Co Ltd, with my kids as shareholders. I knew there would be opportunities to use my entrepreneurial skills in other directions and the new company was to be a vehicle for this. The purpose was not primarily to make money but simply to enjoy the involvement. Enjoying the job and doing it well and not profit had always been the motivating forces in my business life. Profit was simply the evidence that I had succeeded in the other two disciplines. Significantly it was when I abdicated them that things went wrong at Arnotts.

I had a holiday home in Tenerife and often played golf at the challenging Amarilla course in San Miguel de Abona. There was an area of land surrounded on three sides by the course and by the Atlantic Ocean on the other, which I identified as potential for development and I made some enquiries. It had been repossessed by Lloyds Bank and, if it could be acquired at the right price, could prove to be a good investment for some of my share sale proceeds. 30,000 square metres of prime front line land doesn't come cheap so I went into partnership with my old client and very good friend Joe Laidler. We flew to Madrid and after haggling over lunch with the bank's Spanish director, we bought the land. Joe put up the lion's share of the capital. Several years later we sold 9,000 square metres of the land for three times more than we had paid for the lot. We took out our original investment and after paying for the cost of the infrastructure, left the rest in the company to pay for the development of a commercial centre, apartments and a retirement complex on the remaining plots.

Never again will I complain about Spanish lethargy and bureaucracy. By the time we had obtained building licenses the market had crashed before we spent any money on construction. Another piece of good fortune I had at this time was the sale of the properties in my pension fund before prices tumbled. My "retirement" was proving to be not only enjoyable, but quite rewarding – and there had been nothing accidental about that!

With Joe and I in our seventies I don't know whether we will ever get round to developing the land at Amarilla Golf. It may take a long time for the market to improve sufficiently. But we are in no hurry and we may be tempted to sell if the right buyer comes along. If not, the land could be a nice pension fund for our kids. I can still get some business "kicks" helping eldest son James with his property company in South America, but with a recent proliferation of grandchildren I am getting more and more kicks from that direction. This could involve a lot of travelling since the family has acquired a quite international flavour with only youngest son Jacob living in England, the others having settled in Wales, Ireland and South America. With that in mind we are buying another holiday home on the Rochdale Canal in the lovely Calder Valley. Hebden Bridge, with its easy access to transport links may well become our permanent UK summer residence where we can enjoy our retirement in the peaceful tranquillity of this lovely Yorkshire hamlet without worrying about being injured and robbed on the streets as my 85 year old mother was in Middlesbrough.

In between kids and my busy social life I would dearly love to do more writing. Only those who have had a book chosen for publication can empathise with the feelings of pride and satisfaction one experiences when their dedication is recognised and rewarded. Worthwhile becomes all those days of effort (and in my case nights too when flashes of inspiration disturb ones slumber – I am writing this at 3.20 a.m.!).

I am finally devoting less time to business and more to Social, Domestic and Pleasure!

Reflecting on the capricious behaviour of certain people encountered during my lifetime, some of which is described in this narrative, I can think of no better or more appropriate way to summarize my feelings on the matter and to end my story, than to borrow some profound words of wisdom about the human psyche from a poem by Mother Teresa of Calcutta.

THE FINAL ANALYSIS

People are unreasonable, illogical and self centred.
Forgive them anyway.
If you are kind, people may accuse you of ulterior motives.
Be kind anyway.
If you are successful you will win some false friends and some true enemies.
Succeed anyway.
If you are honest and frank, people may cheat you.
Be honest and frank anyway.
What you may spend years building, someone may destroy.
Build anyway.
If you find serenity and happiness, they may be jealous.
Be happy anyway.
The good you do today people may forget tomorrow.
Do good anyway.
Give the world the best you've got anyway.
You see, in the final analysis, it's between you and God; It was never between you and them anyway.

Derrick Arnott
16th July 2011

**Granddaughter Evie Mae Langrell Arnott with her granny
and pops on his 75th birthday.**

Lightning Source UK Ltd.
Milton Keynes UK
UKHW010718010222
398036UK00001B/24